Spiritual Lessons
from
Nature

Rae Karen Hauck

GOLDEN KINGDOM PRESS
DELAND, FLORIDA

Golden Kingdom Press
P.O. Box 1104
DeLand, FL 32721
goldenkingdompress@yahoo.com

ISBN: 978-0-9883280-3-7 (sc)
ISBN: 978-0-9883280-4-4 (e)

Library of Congress Control Number: 2015940840

All photos by Rae Karen Hauck unless noted.

This book is a work of non-fiction.

Printed on acid free paper.

Printed in the United States of America

For my best friend and loving husband, Elliot,
who helped me to see the world differently.

There is a light in you which cannot die;
whose presence is so holy that the world
is sanctified because of you.
All things that live bring gifts to you,
and offer them in
gratitude and gladness at your feet.

The scent of flowers is their gift to you.
The waves bow down before you, and
the trees extend their arms to shield you
from the heat,
and lay their leaves before you on the ground
that you may walk in softness,
while the wind sinks to a whisper round
your holy head.

The light in you is what the universe longs to behold.
All living things are still before you,
for they recognize Who walks with you.
The light you carry is their own.
And thus they see in you their Holiness…
--A COURSE IN MIRACLES

Acknowledgments

To all those nature lovers who have gone before me, leaving a footpath of light in the woods. To the birds, flowers, trees, insects, and animals that were timely messengers. To the angels and nature devas for opening my eyes to a new world. To my dedicated husband, Elliot, for his tireless support and loving inspiration. To my writer/editor friend, Joanna Milton, for her idea to initiate this project. To my grandparents, Walter and Jessie Carpenter, for planting a love of animals in my heart. And, to the Holy Spirit for helping me to see the kinship with all life.

TABLE OF CONTENTS

~Introduction~

*The real voyage of discovery consists
not in seeking new landscapes but
in having new eyes.*
--MARCEL PROUST

I was born with an innate love for nature. My grandparents were Virginia farmers, and time spent on their 200-acre farm as a child nurtured something deep within me. My roots were in that soil, sprouting upward in search of the light. An ancient oak tree stood at the entrance of their land by an Old English-lettered sign *Chesterfield Farm* welcoming visitors. Turning off the paved rural route, barreling down the dirt farm road, cars kicked up a cloud of dust, signaling company was on the way. Grandma always had something good to eat.

Vegetable gardens of green beans, snap peas, lima beans, tomatoes, cucumbers, potatoes, cornfields, pigs, cows, chickens, dogs, and cats were all part of the landscape. An 80-ft. windmill held a 500-gallon wood tank that towered above the old oaks and walnut trees by the white two-story farmhouse. Flat metal blades spun round like petals on a giant pinwheel flower in the sky. Buffeted by many winds, the windmill had stood strong through sleet, snow, blazing summer heat, and soaking rains, pumping water into our lives.

The farm was a place of wonder. My playhouse, a rundown chicken shack, had a premium view of the hog lot where I baked mud pies while the pigs hungrily snorted outside the doublewide window. I loved running barefoot, playing with fuzzy caterpillars, catching fireflies and grasshoppers, weaving clover chain necklaces and picking yellow buttercups to see if anyone liked butter.

Nature was my teacher. Walking around the farm early one day, I had a big surprise. In the ditch along the dirt road, beautiful morning glories were growing wild. Velvety blue blossoms glistened with dewdrops on long green runners in the gulley. Wanting to

1

capture the beauty as my own, I picked a flower off its heart shaped vine, hoping to put it in a vase of water.

Instantly, it wilted in my hand and regretfully I had learned an important lesson. Some things are meant to behold only with our eyes.

Later on in life, Mom liked to tell the story of me as a toddler on the farm. While she was hanging out the wash, I disappeared. Something made her look across the plowed fields. There she saw my blonde head bobbing along the dirt farm road with the cat and dog following in single file. Dust swirled as she came for me in the car. "And where do you think you're going!" Mom asked.

"To see Aunt Lo-Lo," I said. Aunt Lola's house was a half-mile away on the farm. So, at a young age, I was off exploring the world on my own. Mom was surprised that I knew the way, but I was in good company with my animal friends.

Another toddler story that Mom often shared was not as daring. Mom and Grandma heard me crying and carrying on down by the hog lot one day. Puzzled, they found me safely standing by the wire mesh fence. The old milk cow had lowered her brown matted head; two big eyes stared at me from the other side. "Rae Karen? What's the matter!" Mom asked, running to my side.

Too afraid to move, I cried, looking up at the cow's big nostrils. "She's *yookin'* at me!"

Nature is always communicating with us, and when we begin to pay attention, her volume increases. We find our senses are sharpened, and we can understand messages from the animals, the wind, the trees, and all the winged ones. Through nature's myriad colors, scents, shapes, and multitudinous species, she teaches us about our life and the world we live in.

When was the last time you looked up at the stars or took a quiet walk in nature and stopped to watch a bird or admire a flower or a budding tree? When you go into your yard, the park, or spend time in the woods, when you plant a flower or a tree, or when you rescue an animal, free an insect, or honor nature in any way, you are responding to the Spirit in all Life. The world becomes a better place because you cared. Science has learned that humans are not merely observers of our environment, but that our own thoughts, feelings, and judgments actually influence matter for better or worse.

There is a secret waiting to be discovered within the heart of nature. When we let go of believing we as humans are superior, we open ourselves to the experience of living in the community of nature, being part of it, not separate from it. We are welcomed back into the oneness of the Circle of Life.

A Potpourri. . .

~Dreaming of Choices~

Sometimes a lesson from nature may come in a dream. That's what happened to me during a major life change in my forties. A dream carried me back to my grandparents' farm. Usually I dream in color, but this particular one began in black and white. Immediately, from childhood, I recognized the old weathered barn by its cupola on the roof that resembled a cute little house with windows letting in light and fresh air.

An old rooster weathervane on the barn became the focus of my dream. On the weathervane, I had a close-up view of a young sparrow. Amused, I watched the little bird trying to fly. Flapping her wings on the weathervane, she could only spin it around in circles. The harder she tried to fly, the faster the arrow spun round and round, pointing in all directions, with the bird going nowhere.

Then I watched as the dream changed from black and white to living color. My consciousness also shifted from an observer to a participant, where I found myself standing on a ledge of a steep cliff, surveying an expansive vista. Suddenly, when I opened my arms, I found I had wings that extended the length of my entire body. To my surprise, I lifted off the canyon wall, grasping for the boundless sky. Unsteady but airborne, I wondered where to go. The answer came when I spotted a river far below me, winding its way like a narrow ribbon through a patchwork of parceled land. Gliding on air currents, gaining more confidence doing banks and rolls, I headed in that direction.

The two dream vignettes represented choices. Like the sparrow, I could rely on my own power (ego) and try hard to make things happen, pushing out energy in all directions, but getting nowhere. Or, I could let go and soar like an eagle, trusting the wind beneath my wings, as I gained a higher, broader vision of my life's purpose. Like a river must take the land as it comes, I must also learn to bend, and accept situations as they present themselves, knowing that each passage presents a lesson for my soul's growth.

Sometime later, I found this quote in *A Course in Miracles*. The synchronicity summed up the contrasts in my dream of flights.

Who would attempt to fly with
the tiny wings of a sparrow,
when the mighty power of an
eagle has been given him?
--A COURSE IN MIRACLES

~Synchronicity at Work~

No one is where he is by
accident and chance plays
no part in God's plan.
--A COURSE IN MIRACLES

Looking back on fun-filled childhood days, playing kickball, biking, or roller skating on a friend's concrete basement floor as we listened to rock 'n roll records, I remember my girlfriends calling me "Hawkie".

The name seemed to stick throughout life as people often pronounced my last name Hawk instead of Hauck. Little did I know during a transitional time in my adult life, the hawk would become a guiding messenger to a new chapter. The hawk is symbolic of a great messenger, teaching us to become observant of our surroundings— "life is sending us signals!"

One of those signals hit me head-on, changing my perspective on life completely. I had invested twenty years in the security of a government position, slowly climbing up the ladder to supervisor of a team of management analysts at a defense information agency. Through meditation, prayer, and practicing spiritual disciplines, I was being slowly transformed. The material things that had attracted me before no longer held much interest. Just like the caterpillar struggles to fulfill the dream of becoming a butterfly, so was I crystallizing into something more than I presently knew or could understand.

One day at lunch, a close friend made a playful request. Knowing my desire to work at something more fulfilling to my soul, she said to ask the universe for a sign if I was to quit my government job. If it were to be, my friend told me, I would see some sign of a *hawk* at lunchtime while we walked. The universe is a tease and there were several colorful cues: a military bus with the emblem of a hawk on it; or even better, a Thunderbird car parked by the duck pond with my name, KAREN, on the license plate. When lunchtime was over, I returned to my work with the inner promise that I would know when it was time to quit my job, with or without "hawks" to tell me.

After work that day, I had an appointment with my chiropractor to do a Reiki healing on him at his office. I arrived early, and found the waiting area empty. Grabbing a magazine off the stack, I sat down to read. *Virginia Wildlife* had a picture of a large bird hovering near a tree. I found myself wondering if it could be a hawk, but quickly chided myself to give it a rest; it wasn't even lunchtime! Then, opening the magazine at random…I couldn't believe my eyes.

A full-page photo of a hawk, close up, stared at me with the bold caption, "Hawks for Lunch" as a bolt of energy surged through my veins, bristling the hairs on my neck in an explosion of joy.

Turning the page, more hawk photos appeared with the caption, *If you're tired of dreary lunches, take up hawk watching.* The synchronicity was astounding, transcending my understanding. In that incredible moment, I seemed somewhere beyond time and space.

Steps soon came together for me to leave my job and move to Georgia to work on an angel documentary with my brother. I was grateful for the opportunity, as angels had become a part of my experience at the time.

Just as constellations form pictures drawing lines from star to star, so do we connect the dots to unfold the blueprint of our life story. Confirmation was waiting. On my first angel interview, I met a woman who said she too had been guided by a hawk. The hawk also led me to a lovely home in rural Roswell, Georgia. Perhaps this part of my journey was in preparation to becoming a messenger regarding the kinship of all life.

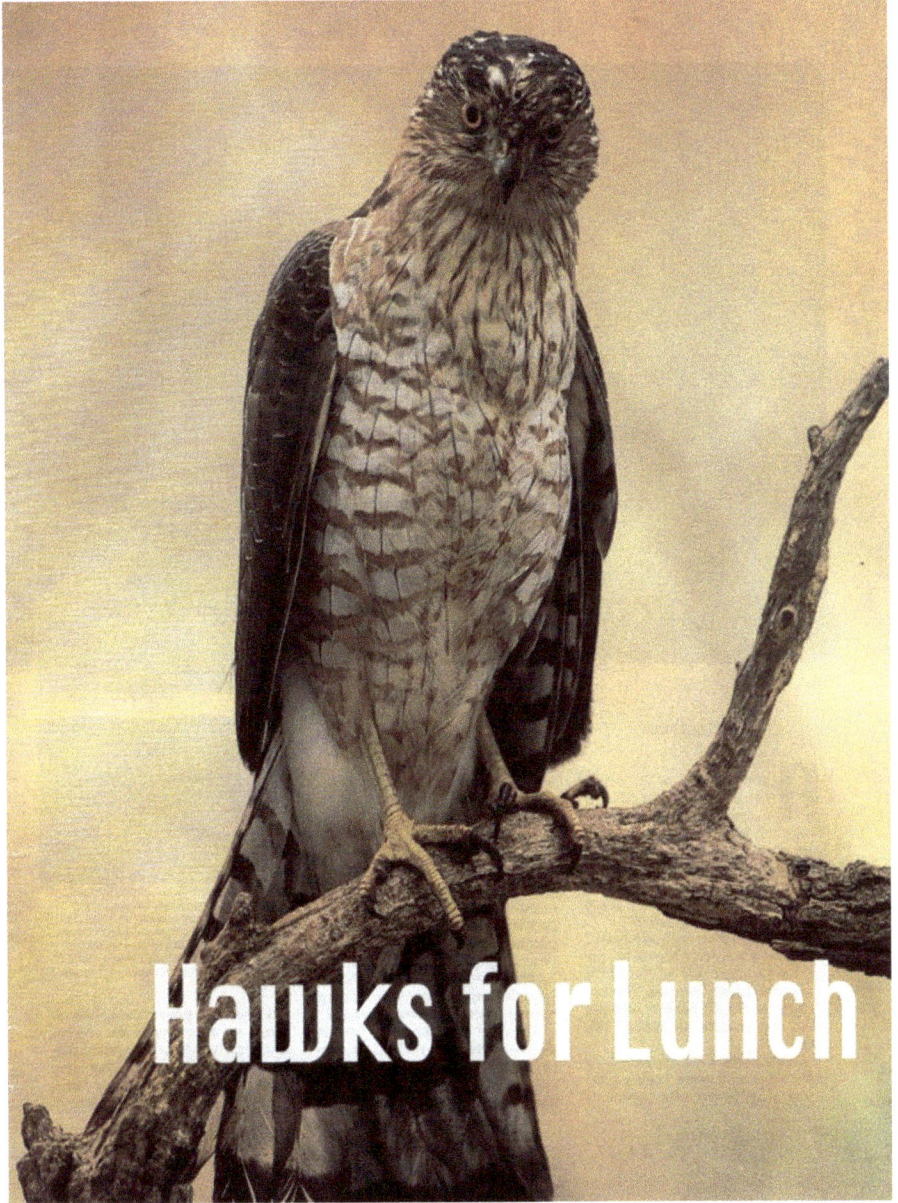

Hawks for Lunch

(Photo: Brian Taber, Virginia Wildlife Magazine)

~Forgive Yourself~

When I moved to Atlanta to work on the angel documentary, my tuxedo cat Schatzi stayed in Virginia with two of my friends. When the move became permanent, a good home was needed for my sweet feline since I would be traveling a lot. A woman named Kim wanted an older cat for her two young daughters. She and I had taken a spiritual class together the previous year. Kim came by the house with her girls to meet Schatzi; it was love at first sight. They took her home that very night. It all happened so quickly as I watched them leave, taking a big piece of my heart.

Two years later, I moved back to Virginia to marry Elliot. Our home was in Kim's neighborhood, but I didn't know her address. On our daily walks, I often wondered where Schatzi lived. Many times, I pictured her in a bubble of white light and sent her love.

A Course in Miracles teaches that we can have a holy relationship with anything we're in relationship with: money, career, partnerships, and of course, our pets. So I asked the Holy Spirit for a holy relationship with Schatzi to heal my guilt over abandoning her to move to Atlanta.

Once we turn a situation over to the Holy Spirit results come, but not in the usual way. Months later, on a walk one Saturday morning, Elliot and I passed a newly painted mailbox. Kim's name was on it! In our comings and goings for the past two years, unknowingly we had passed by Schatzi's house.

The driveway was empty and we stood on the pavement and sent love to Schatzi. The next morning, I returned alone; again, no one was home. I sent light to my cat and thanked her for being such a comfort to me all those years. She was the friendly face that greeted me after work, the one who snuggled with me during challenges and heartaches as I started a new life. I sent her love and asked her to forgive me for letting her go.

That week the Holy Spirit nudged me to go to a new *Course in Miracles* meeting. In the lobby of the healing center, I looked for directions to the *Miracles* meeting. A woman in the outer office at her desk resembled Kim, who had adopted Schatzi, only her hair was short.

Suddenly, she looked up from her paperwork and gave a shout. "Karen! What are YOU doing here?" she cried. "You're supposed to be in Atlanta!" The weirdest expression came over her. "Schatzi died on Sunday. My girls just asked me how I could reach you."

Her words didn't register at first. *Schatzi died?* Then a warm understanding enfolded me. Schatzi had been waiting for me to say goodbye. I told Kim about sending love to Schatzi over the weekend. Her little girls had held a funeral service and buried her by a pine tree in their yard. I was touched and grateful for the loving care my cat had received.

Feeling numb. I found the *Miracles* meeting down the hallway. During the opening meditation, tears suddenly began flowing. I had never taken the time to grieve letting her go. That's just something I do well: stuff my feelings and move on like nothing ever happened. My tears were washing away old walls that blocked me from receiving love. A favorite quote came to mind: *Tears are a sign of a frozen heart melting.*

Later, a facilitator told me, "Kim rarely works here anymore so it's divine timing you came this morning." I realized what a wonderful gift Schatzi had given me with her passing, the gift of knowing love never dies. Love extends beyond time and space. Love is eternal. And, somehow, everything that happened was okay.

~The Housefly~

If your heart is straight with God,
then every creature
will be to you a mirror of life…
No creature is so little or so mean as not
to show forth and represent the goodness of God.
--THOMAS A. KEMPIS

Elliot and I were settling in to go to sleep one night when we heard the buzzing of a fly. Something had to be done about the noisy insect, winging around our room. Years ago, he probably would have gotten the fly swatter and swatted the fly into oblivion. But, today, El admits to knowing so much more about the importance of all life, including insects, that he thought of another plan.

He decided to get a glass and a book, and actually talk to the fly, asking for cooperation. He told the fly, "I will take you to great freedom." If the fly would trust him not to hurt it, he would safely bring the little insect outside. All the fly had to do was go into the glass. Elliot would cover the top with the book, and…

VOILA! out the door it would go to freedom.
Well, Elliot had to talk to this fly for a few minutes. He believed it was going to happen. Really he did.

The fly flew around the area several times, buzzing loudly.

Elliot kept saying to it, "If you get into this glass I'll set you free."

The fly was still not sure so it kept flying and buzzing.

"Enough…already," I said, losing patience.

Elliot asked the Holy Spirit for help.

Soon the fly flew into the glass. What a rush! Quickly covering the glass with the book, Elliot took the fly outside to freedom. He was astonished and happy. So was I.

This is similar to what I believe God is constantly asking us to do. Trust. Listen. Obey. And, then…GREAT FREEDOM.

The story would have ended here, but there is more. You guessed it. Another fly came around when El was writing an article about it for our monthly newsletter, *The Lighthouse of Peace*. Into the glass it flew, upon his request to both the fly and the Holy Spirit.

Once again, great freedom—but, whoops, he flew back inside the house. Elliot finished the newsletter article, and let the fly be.

While stretched out on my stomach reading a book in bed, the fly landed right on my pillow. Slowly tipping the glass on its side, I whispered of freedom, while inching it toward the fly. Having asked for the help of the Holy Spirit, I shouldn't have been so surprised when the fly quickly flew inside. "PRESTO!" Smiling, I covered the glass with my hand, and hurried outside.

Years later, I learned that *fly* brings a message to deal with issues before they get troublesome. This one had taught us another way of problem solving that involved "taking out" our problem in a more loving and respectful manner.

~A Surprise at Stonehenge~

*Your passage through time
and space is not at random. You cannot
but be in the right place at the right
time.*
--A COURSE IN MIRACLES

Visiting a sacred site can be a powerful way of recovering what we may have lost. These unique places are to be seen, touched, listened to, and meditated in, to make a heart connection. Just as we are attracted to different people on a soul level, so are we attracted to certain sacred sites.

Stonehenge, a mysteriously engineered circle of standing and partially fallen stone megaliths, dates back 5,000 years. Elliot and I had an opportunity to visit the ancient stone circle while in England. A British friend provided a special pass for a private viewing before hours. Life is like an initiation and our arrival early that Monday morning was met with a test. An admin error upset the guard. And it had happened with the group ahead of us. I was getting a feeling we might not be admitted when the guard sternly told us to follow him. Silently I asked the Holy Spirit for a holy relationship as we went to his office. I wished him peace on that Monday morning. Before long, a solution was presented, a win-win.

Next my ego worried as we waited for the first group to finish up. Would we get our full hour? The clock was ticking with fear thoughts. I recognized my ego's voice. Getting into Stonehenge wasn't a matter of life or death. It was after all only a *preference.* I realized then that *things* happen because they are supposed to, not because I want them to.

Finally, it was our turn. Heavy rains had been a baptism by water that weekend. Now the sun, a perfect circle framed by two 24-foot grey megaliths, blazed through the haze.

We approached the sacred site by slowly walking in and out, between the 50-ton stones, like a needle stitching its way through time. Some megaliths had stony faces carved by nature. One flat gray boulder on its side looked like a baby whale. Our written prayer requests were placed on top of the rock as we said prayers for friends, family and the world. We invited the Holy Spirit to be with us. A peacefulness settled over the site. Afterwards, we went off to explore on our own.

The grass was green inside the Circle on that gray September morning. I was surprised when Elliot silently motioned, wide-eyed. I couldn't imagine what it was as I tiptoed over.

A brown hare was grazing in the grass in an archway of stones.

To find any animal seemed significant, but what did it mean? The hare didn't run and we respectfully let it be as we continued to explore.

The hour passed quickly and the guard returned to rope off the area. Together we found the hare, gasping in the grass. I crouched down and sent Reiki from a distance. His large eyes looked into mine and he began to relax so much that I thought he may hop into my lap. The guard quietly stood by. He thought the hare was going to be okay. It had probably been attacked by a raptor. I introduced myself.

Elliot joined us and we learned about the guard's childhood stories growing up near Stonehenge. The Holy Spirit had taken a lesson in fear and used it to teach only love.

Years later, I learned more about the symbolism of the hare. It brings a lesson on coming to grips with our deep fears. The hare is always vigilant, ready to take flight—ears perked, wide-eyed. When one crosses your path, it is time to seek out a resting place and find your inner strength by going to the core of your fears and wrestling them to the ground as we are victorious in our spiritual truth.

~Get Up and Go!~

Your new born purpose is nursed by
angels, cherished
by the Holy Spirit and protected by
God Himself.
--A COURSE IN MIRACLES

An airport is a hectic, busy place. Passengers arriving and departing, jets landing, taxiing the tarmac, silver wings queuing up for takeoff, life rolled up in one big crescendo as travelers hustle to their destinations.

When I was younger, I enjoyed flying, that exhilarating feeling of adventure. From my window-seat, I wanted to take in all the sights from here to there. Watching the plane lift from the runway, the dynamic thrust of power made my heart rush to be airborne on a new adventure.

But somewhere along the way, something happened to that eager traveler and I avoided flying anywhere for almost ten years. Then a day came when I had no choice. My husband's aging father had died and plans were made to fly to New York City for the funeral the next day. Boarding the commuter plane, I took a deep breath, remembering angels are God's representatives. Rather than be in fear, I tried to calm my nerves with positive thoughts during the 45-minute flight to Kennedy.

All went well until we hit a pocket of strong turbulence. Gripping the armrest, I closed my eyes, affirming God's angels were enfolding the plane. God is Love, I kept telling myself. A feeling of peace settled over me, clearing my anxious thoughts.

Soon, a beautiful vista of the New York City skyline at sunset greeted me from my plane window like a glimpse of heaven as we smoothly touched down on the runway. Happy to be safely on the ground again, I didn't mind the unusually long delay as we taxied around the tarmac.

Imagine my surprise the next morning to read about the delay in the newspapers. A herd of 150 diamond back terrapins had "stormed" the runways at JFK on their annual pilgrimage to Jamaica Bay to lay their eggs. Human "angels" had helped escort the wayward turtles onto trucks to safely reach their destination. Major airlines had rerouted flights causing delays.

It was a story that gave me hope. I marveled at the internal drive of those pregnant terrapins, lumbering bravely across the tarmac in the path of 747s, sticking out their necks, moving forward to fulfill the call of their life's purpose, to deliver their young. Just like the tortoise won the race with the hare, so did the terrapin win the race with the airlines that day. But humanity was also a winner as airline officials yielded to nature, slowing down advanced technology to meet the needs of motherhood. I loved it.

The message of the terrapin: No matter what the external situation looks like, keep following your own intuition. Help will come to assist you in delivering your creativity to its rightful place. And... it did.

The Beach Years. . .

~Planting Your Energy~

*Faith sees a beautiful blossom
in a bulb, a lovely garden
in a seed, and a giant
oak in an acorn.*
--WILLIAM ARTHUR WARD

A blue heron standing on only one leg on top of a covered bridge at the lake had been the messenger. After going through financial constraints, it was now time to be spiritually more aggressive. We moved back to Virginia Beach where our furniture was in storage, having spent the summer and fall house sitting for a friend in northern Virginia. After several weeks at a hotel efficiency, we landed in an upstairs duplex across the street from the ocean. Our kitchen window had a view of the hill where Edgar Cayce's old Hospital of Enlightenment stood now on the campus of the Association for Research and Enlightenment (A.R.E.). Our involuntary downsizing had become expansive in new and exciting ways. The baby grand piano found a home in the A.R.E. auditorium where Elliot would play for conferences.

Living close to the ocean, powerful dynamics were at work. Our duplex had an eastern exposure. A block from the beach, the constant rhythm of the tides brought a shift in consciousness, a source of rebirth and renewal. The veil is thin along coasts, portals between the world of spirit and the world of human consciousness. The healing energies help to balance the four elements: sun, water, air, and land. The sea holds great mystery. The ocean became a perfect place to find creative and unique approaches to life.

I had once read that the front of one's house represents how the world sees you, while the back represents what's going on behind the scenes. The front and back of our top floor duplex were completely different.

The front faced the service road adjacent to busy Atlantic

Avenue, a hive of activity. The backyard had a window on nature with a 90-ft. long privacy fence, and the shaded shelter of a neighboring old live oak. English ivy grew along the fence, making a lovely natural border. An old brick barbeque grill and patio took up one corner of the property. Our small living space expanded after reading David Daniel Kennedy's book, *Feng Shui for Dummies*. It became life changing for me. Kennedy's advice was all about energy. It doesn't matter if you own or rent your place, invest your energy by honoring nature. So I took up gardening, creating a small flowerbed in the front yard. My downstairs neighbor tried to rain on my enthusiasm with doubts. I was wasting my time, she said. Strong winds, salt air, and sandy soil made it impossible for most flowers to thrive. I decided to think positive and do my best.

Something shifted in the ethers when personal pride in having a beautiful yard was replaced by a desire to co-create beauty for all those who walked by on the service road parallel to busy Atlantic Avenue. With sharing the focus rather than selfish motivation, the universe seemed to open up with an endless bounty. For starters, a friend gave me a heads-up about a nearby house that had been sold and would soon be demolished. Everything was up for rescue: irises, (my favorite flowers) river rocks, bricks—a landscaper's dream come true.

Gardening helped me stay in the now and worry less about financial pressure. I woke up excited; what would unfold in nature today?

In his book, Kennedy also got my attention when I read that our yard reflects the state of our mind. *Could that be true?* Our property owner mowed weekly, but a border of thick bushy weeds landscaped the long fence in the back yard. I decided to take action. With a box of heavy-duty trash bags in one long afternoon, I ripped through that thicket of weeds. I imagined pulling up my own mental weeds by their roots: fear, doubt. anger, guilt. The results were amazing, not only in the yard, but also in me!

Afterwards, I called on the Angel of the Garden for help in

landscaping as I set an intention to honor the earth and co-create with nature. I learned an important lesson on allowing,—not outlining the outcome but staying open as to how the universe would support my intention to share. To my delight, doors opened and even more garden needs poured in like sunshine, despite our limited flower budget. My next-door neighbor, an avid gardener, began sending surplus plants over the fence. Bright-eyed daisies, red vincas, hostas and spidery green-and-white liriope, plus another favorite, little Johnny jump ups; their cute flat petal faces reminded me to smile at life.

The late Thomas Merton in his book, *New Seeds of Contemplation,* had something to say about the many ways God comes to us.

"Every moment and every event of every man's life on earth plants something in his soul. For just as the wind carries thousands of winged seeds, so each moment begins with its germs of spiritual vitality that rest imperceptibly in the minds and hearts of men. Most of these unnumbered seeds perish and are lost, because men are not prepared to receive them: for such seeds as these cannot spring up anywhere except in the good soil of freedom, spontaneity and love."

Nature is abundant. Wild purple violets in our backyard were rescued before mowing day and replanted under the shade of a tree. These dainty flowers were such givers; with long runners, they would send forth new plants. Violets symbolize keeping things simple, lucky opportunities are available. Soon that corner of the garden was colored with purple patches of little violets. I, too, could stretch for new opportunities to share by building upon the old, just like the violets and my neighbor had given so freely.

~The Locust Shell~

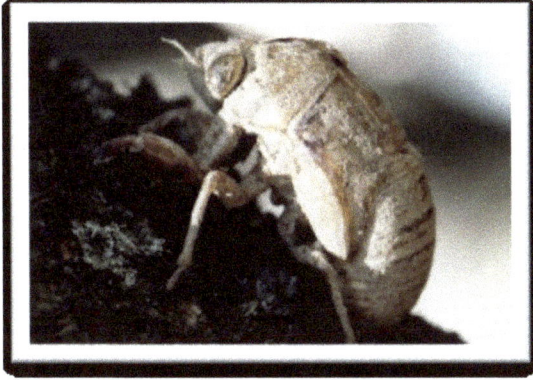

(Photo from Internet)

One evening after a walk, we sat in the backyard enjoying the ocean breeze. Suddenly, Elliot warned me, "There's a strange bug by your chair!"

At my feet, I saw an old familiar sight in the grass, the empty shell of a locust. Picking it up, childhood memories of the farm filled my mind. My brothers and I had collected these shells off the oak trees.

Elliot, born and raised in Brooklyn, was surprised by my calm reaction to the bug. He stared at the skeleton shell, a perfect replica of the prehistoric looking insect, right down to its bulging eyeballs.

His own eyes bugged out as I held it in the palm of my hand, smiling as at an old friend. "Strange to find one here at the beach," I said. "See how the locust pushes out of its old shell, leaving it stuck to a tree?" The locust shell was both creepy and fascinating. The old had been shed for the new.

Finding the locust shell seemed like a deliberate message from nature. In my book *Rise and Shine*. I described feeling hollowed out like a locust shell stuck on an old oak tree. "This is the metaphor I wrote about," I explained, showing Elliot.

"What's it called again?" he asked.

I tried to remember. "Locust... but, it could have been cicada."

Later, I found a photo on the internet that named it both. To my surprise, the site linked to another webpage where I found this message about a locust shell. It was timely, as we had just gone through a letting go process, shedding our old shells to a new life at the beach.

"My child: It's no use being capable if what you achieve is not what I had planned for you. It's no use having a beautiful voice if you sing the wrong song. It's no use writing this, if you don't let my thoughts guide the pen. There is no limit to what I can achieve through you, if you surrender your pride and let me use you in My way. Set aside your daydreams and spend your time aligning your mind to mine, seeking my forgiveness for your willfulness, being open to my guidance.

*You will feel like a **locust** shell, all form and no substance, but as the wind can blow through a locust shell, so the wind of my Spirit can blow through your empty shell, can lift it and set it down in a new place, can make it fruitful beyond your dreams.*

Surrender comes hard, but I ask nothing less. Do not let fear of loss prevent you. I will reward you a hundredfold. When your substance has been surrendered, your form becomes filled with my Spirit. You will be tasting the new wine of my Kingdom. I want this for you. Do not be afraid. I am incapable of acting without love, and your surrender will bring you into My love."

A Message channeled from Jesus (Internet)

~Shedding Old Fears~

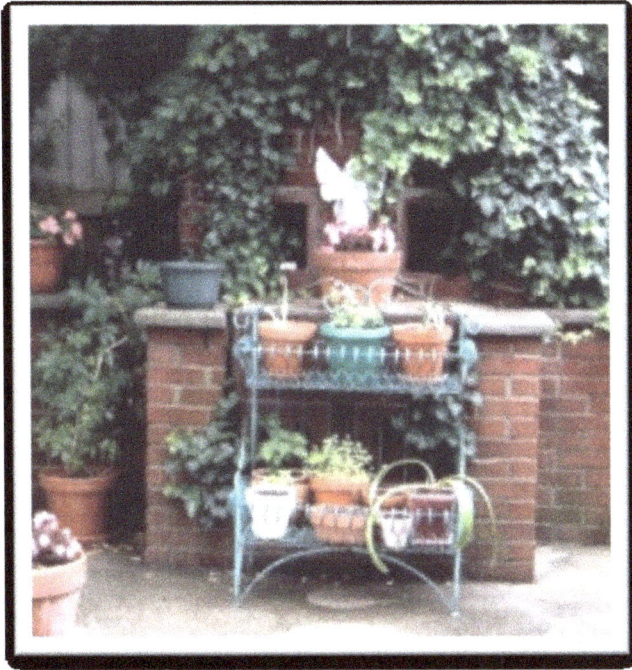

Squirrels, robins, cardinals, and blue jays visited our garden birdbath. Each morning I fed the birds. One unexpected visitor helped me overcome fear. I've always been very frightened of snakes.

I remember from childhood my grandmother, while pruning her roses one day, lifted up her garden rake, shouting, "Snake!"

One look at that long black thing and my young legs took off like a jackrabbit, while Grandma shook with laughter. It turned out I ran from a piece of a garden hose. Fears are often like that, our instinct is to take flight from what we only imagine to be real.

A childhood nightmare about a snake also fed my fear. In the dream, my girlfriend and I were walking home from grade school. Taking a shortcut up the hill behind my house, I was shocked to find my home (the one I lived in at the time) burned to the ground. My family was gone, and as I stood in the smoky yard trying to take it all in, I heard Marguerite yell, "Watch out! A snake!"

Before I could run, I felt its long body slowly wrap around my ankle and slither up my leg. "It's too late," I numbly thought. "I'm going to die." The snake bit me in the neck. I had never died in a dream before. What a relief to wake up the next morning—house intact, family at the breakfast table. It had only been a dream, but it sure felt real while it lasted.

All of this is leading up to a discovery I made in my garden on Atlantic Avenue one morning. While watering the plants, I spotted a long black garden snake in the flowerbed. Having been on a spiritual path, I was slowly learning to see all things with the love of God, so it was to my credit that I didn't scream and run like the wind.

Later, I saw him again in the backyard. To my surprise, the black snake had taken up residence inside the unused brick barbeque grill in the shade of the oak. He had chosen wisely. It had an ivy-laced brick chimney and "wings" to display St. Francis and the Praying Angel of the Garden.

That snake and I had a silent agreement. He would stay away from me, and I would do the same for him. I called him Gardy because he lived in the garden. Although I didn't see him very often, the tip of his black tail sticking out of the barbeque vent made me squirm a little. He had his work to do keeping the yard rodent-free, and I had mine. We had a healthy respect for each other.

Snake represents wisdom; it often reflects transmutation, death, resurrection, and new life. It sheds its old skin in preparation for the new. In looking back, I had gone through a major transformation shedding the old materiality. It hadn't been easy to let go of our two-year stay on the bay, and then live without a home for five months while house-sitting. That whole experience helped me to understand that I am a spiritual being and nothing can take that true spark away from me.

Now in "new skin", I began co-creating with nature in the yard.

I was learning that every plant, animal, flower, and tree has an angel. In a matter of weeks, *our* garden was beginning to emerge as a work of art. My hands would go here or there, and do this or that as if they had a mind of their own Before long, the meditation garden looked like it had been around a long, long time thanks to a little willingness from me to cooperate.

~Letting Love In~

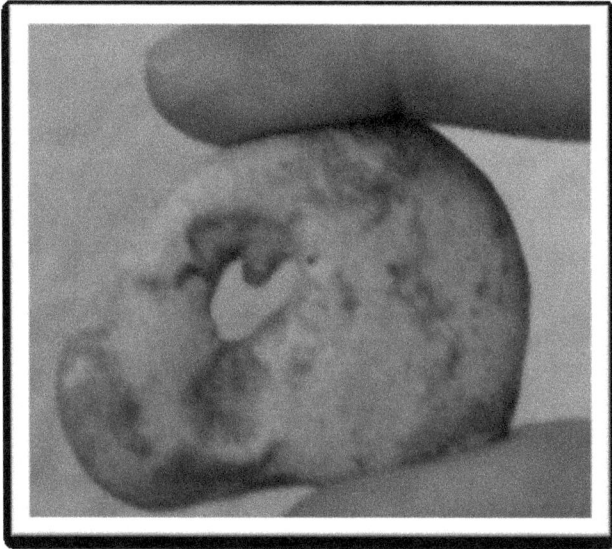

Love waits on welcome,
not on time.
--A COURSE IN MIRACLES

During my sunrise walks, I often filled my pockets with little shells and stones gathered along the beach. One morning I picked up this unusual rock and sleepily tucked it away. It wasn't until I returned home more fully awake that I discovered a hidden treasure while examining my stash. Life is like that sometimes, we don't recognize what we've got until we look more closely. A heart-shaped hole had been naturally carved in the rock. With the small stone, nature was showing me how God's love transforms even the most hardened hearts. It is ever present, and waits on welcome; we only need to let it in.

~The Sunflower~

A sunflower always turns its face toward the sun. That's why these gigantic beauties often symbolize keeping our eyes on the higher Light in whatever we do. A sunflower is not one big blossom as it appears to be, but consists of a cluster of five pointed little flowers, a symbol of organization and teamwork.

I love sunflowers but their tremendous size and beauty were intimidating. So I didn't think about growing my own in the cleared weed patch along the garden wall. Inspiration came while on one of our walks to the park when we passed a house with stately 8-ft tall sunflowers in bloom in the yard. Such tall beauties with rich brown faces and golden crowns commanded attention. One day the owner was in the yard as we walked by. I called out, "What kind are they? They're so big and beautiful."

"Russian," he said, smiling. "Do you want some seeds to grow your own?" Before I could answer, he had broken off a large chunk of a fading flower.

"Oh, I'd better not," I said. "I'm not sure where we'll be living next year."

"Well, you'll be living somewhere, right?" He laughed, giving me the large chunk.

"Yes," I said, thanking him, and I walked home with a warm feeling of carrying a sunflower garden in the palm of my hand.

The next spring, we were still on Atlantic Avenue. I had kept the sunflower seeds in a special envelope over the winter. The space where I had cleared those gangly weeds several years ago became a perfect bed for them.

Tucking in each seed, I called on the Angel of the Sunflowers. Before long, the hard seed broke open and a little sprout wiggled its way to the light. The sunflowers seeds all looked alike, but to my surprise, each one grew at its own pace. Some shorter with a perfect blooming crown, but one in particular had grown the fastest—its thick pole stalk soon towered above the tall stockade fence. This was one was primo. I couldn't wait for it to bloom.

But, then, the strangest thing happened. The beautiful golden crown never opened fully. The others were perfect petite sunflowers, but this giant one remained closed.

It seemed to be a message for not trying to grow too quickly in our spiritual life. The goal is to assimilate and apply the learning gained before shooting up higher and higher. Faster and bigger is not always best. You may gain attention, but not the perfect balance needed to cultivate your natural inner beauty.

~Back in the Swim~

Every dawn promised to be an adventure. On one morning walk, I noticed the beach was spotless; wind and surf had pounded the sand into hard wet pavement with no trace of flotsam or jetsam littering the shore. Walking alone, enjoying the peaceful morning, I was surprised to see something unusual up ahead. I couldn't quite make out what it was but it stuck out like a sore thumb on the empty hard packed sand.

Coming closer, I saw a stranded blue crab. A wave had planted him on the shore. So close to home with no means of getting there, I thought, with compassion for the poor crab. I watched the tide rush inland, its long watery fingers stretching out to grasp his blue shell, but the crab was always just beyond their shallow reach. Silently, I cheered the waves, hoping a powerful one would deliver him home again.

I wanted to help, but feeling the recent effect of a friendly pinch on the ankle, I didn't dare try to pick the crab up. And the usual items to retrieve a crab were swept clean. No sand buckets, plastic shovels, or cups were to be found. I asked the Holy Spirit for help and reluctantly moved on, leaving the crab to his fate. I hadn't gone very far when something made me turn around.

A man and his two big dogs were about to walk by the helpless crab. I wondered, would the dogs hurt him? What a relief to watch them playfully run by without so much as a friendly sniff. Then, I saw the answer to the whole problem: their master had a large shovel over his shoulder!

Hurrying toward them, I saw to my dismay that the man almost stepped on the helpless crab! "Sir!" I called out. "Sir, could you please put that crab back in the sea?"

With a nod, he silently escorted the blue crab on his shovel down to the water's edge. I was pleased that he went beyond the call of duty, wading in far enough to escape the incoming tide. Happily, I watched the crab sail through the air, claws flailing. Splash! *Home at last*. I smiled.

The impossible had happened with a little human intervention. I thanked the crab angel who nodded again, and walked on down the beach with his two frisky dogs.

That experience made me think about my own actions. I had asked the Holy Spirit for help, but I needed to do my part, too, especially when someone comes along with the obvious answer to our prayer.

Before long, I began to "take hold" of a fearful idea that involved public speaking. It was time to come out of my *shell* and share the good news that we are never alone. I volunteered to lecture on the topic of angels at the A.R.E. to remind others and myself that celestial help is always available on our journey home.

~The Legend of the Sand Dollar~

There's a pretty little legend
That I would like to tell
Of the birth and death of Jesus
Found in this lowly shell.
If you examine closely,
You'll see that you will find here
Four nail holes and a fifth one
Made by a Roman's spear.
On one side, the Easter Lily
Its center is the star
That appeared unto the shepherds
And led them from afar.
The Christmas poinsettia
Etched on the other side
Reminds us of His birthday
Our Happy Christmastide.
Now break the center open
And here you will release
The five white doves awaiting
To spread Good Will and Peace.

This simple little symbol,
Christ left for you and me
To help us spread his Gospel
Through all eternity.
--ANONYMOUS

The first time I read *The Legend of the Sand Dollar,* I must admit to being a "doubting Thomas". It was tempting to crack open the beautiful large white sand dollar from an oceanfront gift shop, but it didn't feel right to ruin a thing of beauty for curiosity's sake.

Then, one day I accidentally knocked it off the dresser as I reached for a white feather stuck in my *Course in Miracles* book. Sadly, I picked up the broken shell. A clean break, straight across the top, looked like an opening on an envelope. The accident was such a fluke; I wondered, *Had the Holy Spirit prompted me with the white feather to look inside the shell?* White feathers symbolize the Holy Spirit.

Elliot watched as I carefully cracked open the flat white round shell. *Were there really five white doves inside?* Soon, I held five fragile "doves", little bird-like pieces, in the palm of my hand, each one perfectly formed, with featherlike markings on its tiny wings.

Nature is an amazing teacher. I tucked them inside my God Box where I keep my heartfelt treasures. We thanked the Holy Spirit for helping to free the doves to spread Good Will and Peace at this hour.

~The Donkey Serenade~

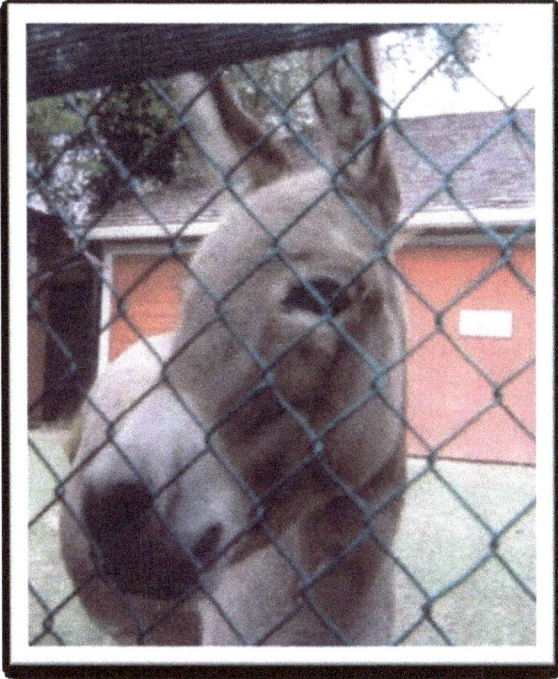

Our voice is a powerful channel for expressing emotions and ideas. If we really want to know how someone feels, we should listen not only to his or her words, but also to the tone of their voice.

At a time in our marriage when funds were low, a favorite past time was spending Sunday afternoons at the Norfolk Zoo. The last hour it remains open free to the public and that fit nicely with our limited budget. I will never forget one Sunday as we sat in the parking lot, waiting for admittance time. I was not in the best of moods. A line from "Breakfast at Tiffany's" fit my description: I had a case of the mean reds, when something is wrong but you're not sure what,— you just don't feel like yourself. Murmuring, I told Elliot to ignore my mood.

No sooner had I said that when I heard a loud raucous call coming from a nearby animal pen. It seemed to mimic my disposition so much that we laughed. Chasing away the mean reds, we hurried to see where the sound came from.

Braying loudly in her outside pen, Katie, our donkey friend was looking out through the fence. The nylon netting had slipped down so she could stick her nose through the links to get closer to us. "Katie, you're so special," we said, showering her with attention.

Playfully Elliot began singing *The Donkey Serenade to her,* a song he learned in the 5th grade. After a few verses, there is a part in the song where the donkey sings back. Elliot looked at Katie, "Girl, this is where you come in," he said, waving his hand like a showman. He gave her a cue, "E-e-aw."

Katie performed like a star— ears pent back, nostrils flared— braying loudly, "E-E-AWWWWWWWW..."

A group of giggling children from the parking lot came over to hear this odd duet. Katie kept on singing, enjoying the attention. Afterwards, everyone agreed that we had shared something special.

The next day, we returned to the zoo for a picture of Katie to put in our *Lighthouse of Peace* newsletter. To our surprise, the caretaker wouldn't let us near Katie. When I told her about Sunday's duet and how loving the little donkey had been, the young woman looked at me surprised. "Loving is not a word I would use to describe *her*," she said with a faint smile. "She kicks and bites."

The caretaker took a long shot photo of Katie, but it didn't capture her sweet face.

On our way to the parking lot, we saw Katie in her pen. The netting was down, and we called her to come over to the fence. She ran to greet us and again we showered her with love and took this picture. She gave us a friendly goodbye bray. We had learned another lesson on teaching only love.

Later, I learned that *donkey* represents the art of being humble and waiting for recognition, like the lowly donkey that carried the Master into Jerusalem on Palm Sunday. The message of the donkey is, don't go blowing your own horn, wait for the opportunity to present itself to you, like Katie had one Sunday afternoon at the back entrance to the zoo, when she had her moment to shine like a star.

~The Love Envelope~

The universe of love does not
stop because you do not see it,
nor have your closed eyes lost the ability
to see.
--A COURSE IN MIRACLES

Saint Francis, The Patron Saint of Animals, opened my eyes to seeing God in all of life. He believed that everything that existed, from angels to insects to rocks, was part of his dear family. He taught God's love through the creatures around him. All were his brothers and sisters. They seemed to recognize this and flocked to him.

While living at the beach on Atlantic Avenue, an army of ants had set up camp in our kitchen. Not wanting to kill them, Elliot had a plan. He placed an envelope on the countertop and put a dab of honey on it. When the ants gathered, he would then escort them outside. My friend Debra was scheduled to pay us a visit, and preparing for our guest we decided to let the ants just be. Ants teach us how to work in a community to achieve our goals. They also can symbolize patience. I was hoping by now I had enough.

Later, when I returned to the kitchen, the ants had gathered on the envelope, but their formation seemed so deliberate, it caught me by surprise. Surrounding the dab of honey, sipping it side by side, they had formed a wide heart on the envelope! I ran to show Elliot.

"Love is the answer," he said, watching them enjoy the nectar of life.

Elliot had mentioned showing Debra the ants, but I kept the kitchen door closed during her tour. Later, my friend got up from the sofa with her empty glass. "You didn't show me your kitchen," she said.

Rather than have her think I was a messy housekeeper, we let her see the ant situation. Besides, I thought it would be good to have another witness as I was having a hard time believing it myself.

In amazement, we watched the love squad of ants sipping honey in formation. In that incredible moment, I realized that I do not know the real meaning of anything, but it did seem to be a message about having patience with love. There is an abundance for all, so share.

J. Allen Boone, in his book *Kinship with All Life,* explains that there is only one Consciousness, whether it is on the human level or animal level or other. We are all one Consciousness. And, the moment we learn to make contact with each other, love enters into our experience and we are transformed, having gone beyond *form* into *substance* of being *One.* Thanks to the ants, we had learned an important lesson on seeing Life through a lens of Love.

Prayer of Saint Francis of Assisi

Lord, make me an instrument of your peace.
Where there is hatred, let me sow love.
Where there is injury, let me sow pardon.
Where there is doubt, let me sow faith.
Where there is despair, let me sow hope.
Where there is darkness, let me sow light.
Where there is sadness, let me sow joy.
O Divine Master, grant that
I may not so much seek
To be consoled as to console.
To be understood as to understand,
To be loved as to love.
For it is in giving that we receive.
It is in the pardoning that we are pardoned.
It is in dying that we are born to eternal life.

~The Humpback Whale~

(Photo: Backflip, Gregory T. Chaly)

Walking at the water's edge, heading south on the beach, I was not fully awake one sunrise when a large gray mammal swam near me. To my surprise, the mammal kept up with my pace, and my heart skipped in hopes of fulfilling a dream to see a whale. I had surrendered my thought to the probability that it was a large dolphin when suddenly a blast from a blowhole showered my expectations with joy as I saw a baby humpback whale!

Soon I discovered a reunion was happening in the ocean by the Ramada Inn, where an enamored group of souls gathered to enjoy this welcome but surprise visit by a family of humpbacks.

Although I didn't get a picture, a framed photograph, entitled, *Backflip* surfaced at a thrift shop in Virginia Beach a short time later. It displayed the dynamic power needed to "flip" his floating tonnage. And yet it happens! Suddenly inspiration surges, fueled by enthusiasm, and the humpback soars on "wings" from the realm of sea to blue sky in a single flip! A brand new perception that forever

47

changes a paradigm.

Whales are magnificent creatures. Their song is powerful, traveling under the ocean for thousands of miles. Whales teach us to sing our own song. We are each unique and bring gifts to share with the world. Whales will occasionally breach, coming completely out of the water. When they do, it is important to ask: How am I using my creative ability? Am I keeping everything inside in fear of letting it out? If so, it's time to breach and reveal the magnificence and power of your own creativity. Do not hold back.

~Sunglow~

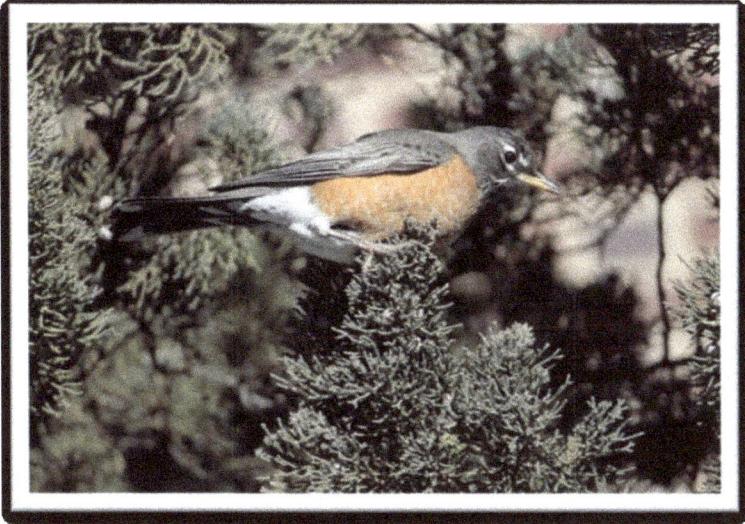

(Photo from Internet)

Teach me to listen to
the song of the Earth.
--UNKNOWN

An unexpected blizzard delivered chunks of hail on the lower roof of the duplex. Just last week, the temperature had been in the 80s at the beach. This sudden cold spell probably made our feathered friends wonder, what happened to spring?

I watched a lone robin atop the old fence post, staring at the sun reflected in his shiny eye. Facing east, his talons dug into the wood as he swayed in the winds that ruffled his feathery red breast. From time to time, he seemed to puff up his chest like a down-winter coat for added warmth.

Robins do puff up their chests and sing loudly when arguing over territory. Their "battles" are in song, but that bitter cold morning, harmony was in the air as I watched dozens of red robins land on the sprawling live oak. They gathered in perfect symmetry, brightening the bare tree branches in red, like bright ornaments on a

Christmas tree. I had never seen so many robins gather in one place. A fable tells of how a robin tried to pull the thorns from the head of Christ on the cross and was stained by his blood, and that's why it has a red breast. I said a prayer that our yard would be a haven for all the birds that day, asking the Holy Spirit to watch over them and keep their little bodies warm.

An idea came to serenade the waiting flock. I asked Elliot to play a song for them. He laughed, and said, why not? Moving the keyboard closer, he raised the window. A cold blast swept the warm room. His choice of music was *Sunglow*, a tune he had recently written.

More robins began gathering on the old tree, enjoying his song as they faced east, looking in Elliot's direction.

When the concert was over, robins began pecking at the ice chunks on the roof to quench their thirst. A flock of cedar waxwings joined in the ice-breaking festivities. These yellow-breasted birds with their crested heads and black masks landed in pairs, their dainty feathers shivered in the wind. The song of the cedar waxwings I knew well: "I see. I see. I see." It was a reminder of my favorite hymn, *Amazing Grace*. *"I once was blind, but now I see."* With the help of the Holy Spirit, thankfully I can change how I see the world.

In you is all of Heaven.
Every leaf that falls is given life in you.
Each bird that ever sang will sing again
in you.
And every flower that ever bloomed
has saved its perfume and its loveliness
for you.
--A COURSE IN MIRACLES

~Footstool~

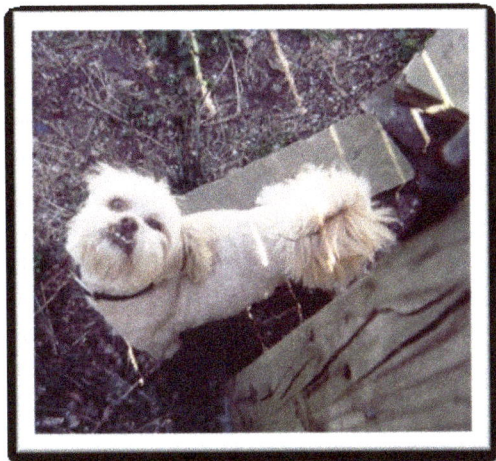

One sunny afternoon, following a visit to the state park, Elliot and I took a short-cut home. On the way, a small dog in need of a friend caught our attention. His short legs paced up and down by a house with a fenced-in yard.

Spotting us, he ran toward me. I wasn't sure if he was friendly, but choosing to come from love, I bent down and extended my hand for a lick. Looking up with warm amber eyes, he wagged his tail. This dog was a sweetheart.

Having recently read a book on animal communications, I confessed that I wished I could understand you better. *Is this your home?*

No cars were in the driveway, but this little fellow appeared to be locked out of his own yard by mistake. I vaguely recalled a furry ball barking at us last year when we asked about a desk on the curb for give-away. Thinking about it, I was 99 percent sure this was the same dog...until I peeked over the fence. A big dog was basking in the sun on the front walk! Neither one barked, a good sign, but now I wasn't sure what to do.

Leaving this little one in the care of the angels, I decided to call his owners, evidently local chiropractors, judging from the bumper sticker I'd seen on their car during previous walks to the park. At home, I called their office; the receptionist said it sounded just like their dog, Footstool. Would we escort him back inside the gate?

Happy to help, we quickly drove back to get Footstool. He hadn't strayed, but was patiently waiting by the gate. As we pulled up, a man had just walked by with his pit bull on a leash. Footstool was so excited, he ran toward his fence, cocking his head, showing me the way.

"You're going home!" I said, swinging open the gate.

Hurrying inside, he paused and turned around as if to say, "Whew! There's no place like home. Thank you!"

I thought about the lesson Footstool had taught me that day. He kept his focus on the goal, home. He hadn't wandered off to the nearby park. Loyal, he patiently waited outside the gate, knowing eventually the door would swing open, and he would return to his kingdom.

A few days later, "Footstool" appeared again. This time I read the word in a Bible passage where the Lord says, "...the earth is his footstool." The synchronicity brought a smile. After all, it's only a matter of time until we return to the kingdom *within*. Watch, wait, and pray, like Footstool.

~A Special Delivery~

There is coming a sounding
forth of new life, like the trumpeting
on a conch shell.
Prepare for journeys to a
new and protected life.
--TED ANDREWS

When I worked for the government, I made an interesting trade with a friend, a deep-sea diver. His gigantic razorback clamshell for my large shark tooth seemed like a great bargain. Later, I learned that gifts from the sea can be delivered in unexpected ways.

On my early morning beach walks, I would invite Jesus along. I was living in the midst of two extremes: the abundance of the sun, surf, and sky, and the limited resources in our bank account. During those lean years, I was learning the gift of gratitude for everything: the water I bathed in, the food I ate, the time for contemplation, and the love of my family.

Each dawn carried a message to be revealed along the way.

Often I would stop and pick up little glistening shells on the wet sand. Since our finances were low, I wanted the reassurance that God still loved me. I set an intention to find a perfectly large conch shell, a gift from the sea. But, the shells that had washed up were mostly flawed. Time went on and soon my request was forgotten.

One morning, a year or so later, as I walked barefoot in the shallow surf, a powerful wave rushed in and rolled back the sea, giving me a clear view of the ocean floor.

Bubbles emerged at my feet.

A tip of a shell stuck out in the watery sand! Pulling it up, I smiled. "Thank you, Holy Spirit!" I whispered, gazing at the biggest conch shell I'd ever seen at the beach. Although the outer shell was dark, the inside was glossy orange, like new. The large vessel had once been home to a conch that had moved on to bigger things.

I hadn't walked very far when more bubbles appeared by my feet. I was amazed! Now, I held two extra large conches, almost identical in color and size. I laughed, one for me and one for Elliot.

I fondly remembered an old conch shell Grandma had on her porch. "Listen," she told me when I was a child. "Hold it by your ear." I laughed, feeling silly, but what a rush to hear the surf like magic to my young ear.

My "special double for your trouble conch delivery" had come when I needed it most. The outgoing tide had revealed what had been buried from sight. Later as I listened to my gift at home, it may have been my imagination, but I heard, "The tides are rushing in with new beginnings. You can hear it, when you choose to be still and listen."

The Farm Years. . .

~The Apple Tree Lady~

(Profile inside circle)

Look deep into nature,
and then you will
understand everything better.
--ALBERT EINSTEIN

Seven years of co-creating with nature on busy Atlantic Avenue turned out to be a stepping-stone to a cottage rental on a ten-acre farm near Sandbridge Beach, a perfect setting to overcome any fears of things that creep and crawl.

Something wonderful happens when living close to nature, especially on cool evenings, when you can sleep with the sliding glass doors open and tune in.

Shortly after moving to the farm, I was awakened in the middle of the night. My senses were heightened at the abundance of nature surrounding our little home. I could actually sense the grass growing, the trees budding, and the flowers blooming. As I lay there in the ecstasy of springtime, I saw the moon aglow. It seemed to rise like an orange halo on the blossoming old apple tree. The tree's sweet essence wafted through the night air.

This resurrection energy was so palpable. My emotions overflowed in joyful tears. The serenity here was such a contrast from the constant traffic on Atlantic Avenue. I tuned in to the pond, listening to bullfrogs croaking like Tibetan monks chanting, and soon fell back to a restful sleep.

In time, that old apple tree and I became good friends. I would see her from my bed first thing in the morning as I emptied my mind. Gazing out the bedroom slider, my thoughts could stretch beyond the golden fields and green pastures carrying me like a leaf riding the wind.

I watched the old tree transform that first spring. When her lovely apple blossoms faded, green "pearls" nestled in her shiny new leaves. By the end of her season, she had spread out a feast for the birds, squirrels, and other creatures to enjoy.

With the help of the nature divas, I created a meditation garden and included that tree in the design. My tall garden praying angel stood in a bed of pink impatiens underneath her leafy full branches. One day while weeding, a large perfect apple landed beside me. I smiled, accepting the invitation to share. Thanking my tree friend, I took a bite, officially sealing our bond of friendship.

Then, in the fall, she loosened her leafy coat and stood bare. Her gray weathered trunk and twisted empty limbs held no trace of her beauty. Once soft and lacey in flowering pink like a blushing bride carrying a fragrant bouquet, now she was resting in a dream of spring.

Then, one winter's morn, as I gazed at her from my bed, I was startled to find something new and different. The old tree's twiggy branches had naturally formed a profile of a lady's smiling face as if fashioned by the old apple tree herself!

This childlike discovery filled me with wonder as if finding a hidden object in a children's picture book. The smiling face looked to the east, to the sunrise, a place of illumination and new beginnings. That long winter I became rather fond of her image.

But, with the return of spring, I bid her a fond farewell as she disappeared in a tapestry of new green leaves. The weight of the apples, and squirrels that scampered on her limbs would surely break up her twiggy profile.

But, I was wrong.

Following a plentiful harvest, the wind tossed her leaves until she again stood in her nakedness. One winter's morning, I opened my eyes. Glancing upward, I saw her. The Apple Tree Lady was still there!

I knew she was teaching me many lessons: How life brings changes and things once seen can disappear for a season, but although no longer visible, they remain with us to return again bringing a gift of wisdom in the divine order of all life.

Our bond continued, but the following autumn, I really didn't expect to see her face again.

But, once more, I was wrong.

It was as if the old tree and I shared a secret joy, like finding a long lost friend.

See me! I made it! was her message. *There are many hidden mysteries yet to be revealed. Do not be deceived by the many changes that shroud your view. Things are not always as they appear. You, too, have an inward Spirit that is untouched by life's circumstances.*

I marveled at the seasons she had weathered to bring her full circle again. Then, during a winter storm, a blanket of powdery white snow covered her branches. Admiring the lovely picture of serenity, I took pictures from my window knowing she was gone from the weight of the wet snow.

But, I was wrong, again.

When sun and wind had swept her clean, the Apple Tree Lady was still there, a little worse for wear, but still smiling. I thanked her for teaching me the gift of patience and perseverance through grace during the seasons of life.

Fascinated by the spirit of this old tree, I looked up the symbolism of apple. It represents wisdom. When you cut an apple crosswise, you'll find the seeds radiate in the shape of a five-pointed star, a sign of hidden knowledge.

Even more interesting, in *Nature-Speak*, Ted Andrews writes:

"The apple tree is a loving giver, especially when treated with love and respect by humans. It thrives on human contact and teaches the power of sharing. It often heralds contact with spirit and especially contact with the Faerie Realm."

I am forever thankful to my apple tree friend for her playful, giving, gentle spirit. "If nature is your teacher, you will truly learn."

~The Deer Dream~

Each day, each hour, every instant, I am
choosing what I want to look upon,
the sounds I want to hear, the witnesses
to what I want to be the truth for me.
--A COURSE IN MIRACLES

A vivid dream about feeding a young deer came to me shortly after moving to the farm. This gentle tawny creature was eating an apple from my hand in a tender moment of trust. The next morning, I woke up with a feeling of innocence. Living in Virginia Beach for nine years, I had yet to see a deer, so I didn't think much about it.

A few months later, when the apples were in, our property owner asked if we had seen the deer come to eat from the old apple tree. The white tailed deer return through a wooded opening at the back edge of our rental property. I was impressed that my dream had been somewhat prophetic.

I looked forward to their arrival, but it was soon forgotten, as we had to take a long road trip to visit family in New York. Arriving home after ten days, I enjoyed a nap in the comfort of our own bed. Waking up energized, I found myself rearranging the bed to face the sliding glass doors. That night I turned in early, after my cleaning frenzy. The sun was slowly setting in that magical hour of dusk when the veil is often the thinnest. Gazing out at the meditation garden, the expansive country view was healing to my senses: golden fields, pond, heavy plow, woods, and the old apple tree.

My revelry was enhanced as out of the corner of my eye I caught sight of a beautiful tawny doe as she quietly emerged from the woods. With a graceful step, she made her way slowly down the garden path. Stopping, she paused to nibble on blades of grass. Only the screened patio door separated us and I scarcely took a breath not wanting to frighten her. While we had been away, she must have enjoyed the freedom of visiting the apple tree. Now, it would be as much of a surprise to her as she was to me if I made a bold move.

I watched in wonder as her big brown eyes looked around before bowing her head and chomping on the fruit that lay at her feet by the old tree.

Never having seen deer up close, I was entranced by her gentle manner and wide-eyed innocence. I wondered why anyone would want to harm such a gentle creature. In awe, I watched her delicately chew on the apples. It was nightfall when she finished eating and moved to the far side of the tree, no longer in view. I soon fell into a peaceful sleep.

After midnight, a burst of expectancy woke me. I bolted upright in bed, looking out the slider. A subtle movement near the apple tree made me wonder, had the deer returned for a midnight snack? To see her twice in one evening seemed too good to be true.

Then like magic, the moon shifted from behind a cloud shedding light on the old apple tree. A still silhouette of the deer appeared in the moonlight. Her gentle presence touched a wellspring of unexpected tears from some long forgotten place within my heart.

Was it a cry for the lost innocence in the world, or a disconnect from the sanctity of all life?

I only know the depth of that emotion caught me by surprise. The Holy Spirit seemed very close in that perfect moment, knowing how to heal my heart. I know some will say that all moments are perfect, and they are. It is only our perception that clouds the miracles. But, this deer had come to heal the aching in my heart. I still have emotions that make this journey wearisome at times. *A Course in Miracles* teaches that it is a journey without distance to a place we never left. Sharing our problems with the Holy Spirit, He will translate them into Light.

Soon, I drifted into a peaceful sleep, remembering *deer* represent gently being guided on a new adventure. Living on the farm was opening up an exciting new kinship with all Life.

~Heart and Hands~

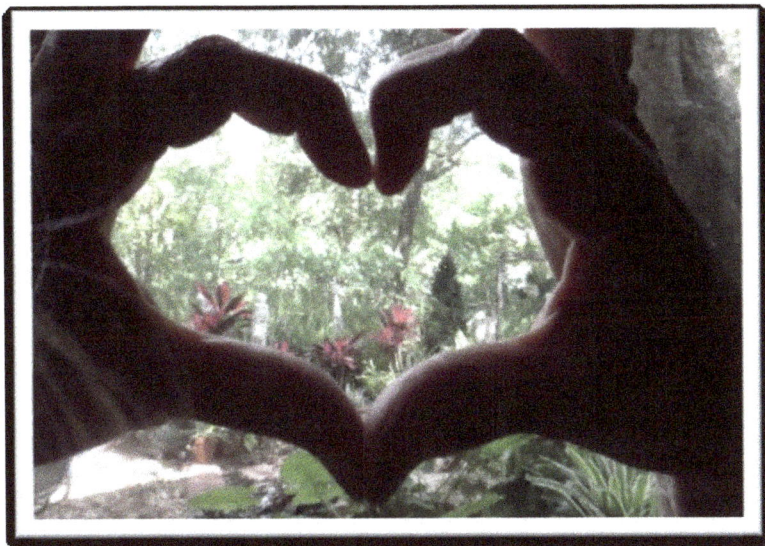

Unable to sleep one night at the cottage, I got up and grabbed a book on healing. The Chinese believe that hands are an extension of the heart, and since the heart is considered to be the seat of the Mind, it is understandable that gentle and harmonious gestures reflect a peaceful heart. Likewise, a disturbed Heart (Mind) is the underlying cause behind aggressive, agitated, and uncontrolled hand movement.

While reading some spiritual material by Emmet Fox published in the 1930s, I came across a unique example of oneness in your hand. If you look at your hand with your palm facing you, you will understand the answer to all of life's questions. Look at your fingers as representing different people, all kinds of people from anywhere on earth. See how they are separate from each other physically. Now, notice they are all connected to the palm. The palm represents God, or the All That Is.

What a marvelous recognition to see how everyone is connected to the one God. Even though we may appear separate in materiality, we are really all connected spiritually. Our bodies are only projections of our true self. That is not who we really are. It is sometimes difficult to remember this, but the reminder is in the palm of your hand.

When you feel rejected in any way, look at your hand. When you need the strength of God to help carry you through a trial, look at your hand. There really is no separation even though it may appear to be. If you need to confront someone about an issue, look at your hand. Try to let it remind you of our oneness with each other. That is the answer to all problems. God is love.

Our journey here is to remember that *God is* and we are one with Him. Nothing else is really going on. When we look to lend a helping hand, remember that it is God in action.

Our hands look like angel wings when both palms are facing down, thumbs joining together, fingers touching. In my morning meditation, I reflected on the many ways I use my hands, without any thought of gratitude. I welcome each new day by feeding my bird friends as I call out, "Good morning, God! I love you! This is Rae Karen."

That morning, young cardinals were waiting in the garden. I got up, filled the birdseed tray, and returned to bed to watch the show. Suddenly the many birds and squirrels scattered at once. Then I saw Junior, my Bambi boy. His antlers had grown. He stood near the far side of the tree. I could only get a glimpse of his mouth or his antlers, every now and then. But he was there by the tree trunk. His shadow cast a peaceful hush in the early morning sunlight. I thought how his presence is a lot like God's. You know He is always here, but you catch glimpses of Him in the physical, like God winks.

"Bambi" came out from behind the apple tree. His tawny coat, strong spindly legs, swishing white tail added to his charm. I watched him bite into a whole apple, dropping half of it on the ground, as he backed up and went after it again. I found myself praying that this gentle creature would be protected, grow strong, and have many babies. I caught a gleam of sunshine in those brown eyes as he lowered his head to eat.

Then, with belly full, he turned and in great dignity walked back toward the woods. He was a prince and I enjoyed serving him. Thankfully, I had gathered fallen apples and spread them in the yard for a feast.

Later, I opened my *A Course in Miracles* book at random. I smiled at the passage as I read about the hand of Christ being all there is to hold:

"...Christ's hand holds all His brothers in Himself. He gives them vision for their sightless eyes, and sings to them of Heaven... He reaches through them, holding out His hand, that everyone may bless all living things and see their holiness."

~The Call of the Geese~

Sometimes Nature will lend a helping hand. I fondly recall a memory while living on the farm. Elliot and I took a break from work and went for a drive in the countryside exploring new territory. I brought my camera and set an intention that we were on a photo safari. Nature would reveal the animals along the way. Although a peaceful ride by farms and open pastures, there was no sign of any wildlife. Time passed and my prospects looked dim.

Randomly turning down a long narrow country road, we hit pay dirt, amazed by hundreds and hundreds of large white birds that suddenly drifted out of a gray sky. They dropped like manna from heaven, blanketing a barren field as white as snow. But I had regrettably missed a perfect action shot. Watching them gather, we listened to their loud cacophony, enjoying their noisy convention from the roadside.

With a special love for geese, I decided to slowly cross the wet field to take a photo, from a respectful distance. The nearer I came, the louder the chatter. I stopped and sent love. Suddenly a blizzard of thunderous wings flapped, stirring the air in magnificent flight. What a rush as I stood still, my feet slanted on the earth but lifted upward by their dynamic thrust.

Later I learned that geese are a totem to help in communicating through the use of stories, like Mother Goose. Their feathers were also used as writing quills in the past. When geese appear, they can help us move through any creative blocks, and they did.

Geese also invite us to heed the call to the quest.

~Fully Rely on God~

It was dusk as I hurried to empty the trash outside the cottage. Popping open the large garbage lid, I was surprised to find a cute little tree frog clinging near the top wall, in need of rescue! "I'll help you," I said, looking around for a short stick to escort him out. I held the stick by his tiny green feet, coaching him. "Let go and climb aboard."

But his little eyes stared at me without blinking. He was too afraid to take that leap, even though I kept assuring him of my good intentions.

Then, he did it.

He took a big leap—only in the wrong direction, and disappeared under a pile of large plastic trash bags.

Now what? I wondered.

In good conscience, I couldn't shut the lid and leave him trapped overnight. And, out in the country, other critters would have a real picnic if I left the lid open.

Almost sundown, I had to do something!

Stretching my arm down inside the industrial tank, I tried moving the trash bags, but they were just beyond my grasp.

An "angel thought" came to find something to shift the bags. Nearby on the ground, I found a perfect stick, lightweight and long, with a bonus! Two twig-like prongs, perfect for bag fishing. I asked the Holy Spirit and the angels for help.

I lowered the stick and caught a bag right away. Slowly raising it up, I had a good laugh. The angels must have been helping because the little green tree frog was clinging to that very bag! Like a gentleman, he rode it all the way out of the trash can.

"Thank you, Angels," I said, quickly, putting the bag down. "You're free!" I told my passenger.

To my surprise, his green fingers and toes had tiny round discs, like suction cups, that stuck tight to the bag.

"You're free!" I told him again. "You can go!"

With daylight fading, I was becoming impatient as I moved him and the bag closer to nature by the old walnut tree. "Please, go," I told him.

But he stubbornly stayed on his trash bag. It took some gentle prodding before he leaped away on a new adventure.

Watching him disappear in the grass, I thought about his lesson. Sometimes you may find yourself stuck in a mess with no way out. The key to freedom is to Fully Rely On God (acronym for F.R.O.G.) and to do your best to climb above your heap of troubles. Wait there patiently for help; an unexpected way *will* open up. And when it does, do not be afraid, but move forward. And...most of all, remember... let go of your old garbage and take a leap of faith in a new direction.

A month later, an unusual visitor came calling at the cottage. "Hurry! You've got to see this!" Elliot shouted, "A frog's at the front door! His hands are folded in prayer!"

This little tree frog was clinging to the windowpane like a patient gentleman caller. "Are you the one I rescued from the trash several months ago?" I playfully asked.

Just as a frog goes through a metamorphosis, maybe he was a symbol of coming into our own creative power. A frog transforms in three stages: an egg, to a polliwog, and finally to a frog. With all the major global transformation, frog brings a strong message to **F**ully **R**ely **o**n **G**od. Stay in your "center" and don't be deceived by appearances as humanity prepares to take a quantum leap to a higher state of consciousness. Our darkest hours can lead to our brightest new days.

~Reflections~

Life is a mirror peopled by many selves
Wish I could love those I don't
then I would love myself.
--MARIAN GORDON

In Kabbalah, our physical world is a reflection of the endless world, and comprises only 1% of our true reality. Everything we do stirs up a corresponding energy in other realms of reality. The understanding that our actions, words, and thoughts set up a reverberation that unfolds in the universe moment by moment is important, as all the variables leading up to that one moment impact the outcome. Because everything is inter-related, when we become mindful in what we say or think, we understand that a seemingly insignificant gesture or word could have a heavy consequence in that moment.

I was "reflecting" on reflections while soaking in the tub one morning when something caught my eye in the mirror over the bathroom sink. A Granddaddy Long Legs spider slowly lowered himself stroke by stroke from the white ceiling.

A fine thread of his own making gave him endless opportunities to create in whatever direction or design he desired. Seeing him first in the mirror, I wondered if he could see the reflection of his creation in the looking glass.

Had he come to teach me to watch what I'm weaving with my own thoughts out in the world?

Daddy Long Legs symbolizes the weaving of deeper relationships. Relationships are a mirror as to how well we are doing in overcoming our ego. What are our loved ones and significant friends reflecting to us? No one is in our life by chance; those closest to us are designated to be here to help us fulfill our life's purpose and we for them. If we do not work through issues as they arise in our relationships, the avoidance only binds us with an even tighter thread to that same sticky situation, over and over again until we finally learn our lesson.

It is helpful to remember that we also have a personal relationship with the world of maya (illusion) that can be compared to a universal mirror. All minds are joined, and in reality, there are no private thoughts. Whatever or whomever we dwell on in our consciousness is reflected and *magnified* in the physical world around us. It is as if our own inner thoughts are as obvious as parading a big purple polka dotted elephant through a fun house hall of mirrors. That vivid image is multiplied many times over, making a lasting impression until we make the effort to change our mind.

~The "I Love You" Game~

(Photo from Internet)

To those who in love of Nature
hold Communion with Her visible
forms, She speaks a various language.
--WILLIAM CULLEN BRYANT

Sometimes if we are too attached to how other people perceive us, a lesson will present itself in the most amusing way. Freedom is being able to express yourself in the moment without any fear of ridicule or judgment, and be the playful, loving, spirit that God intended you to be.

On our way to and from the cottage on the farm, the Virginia Beach Aquarium on General Booth Boulevard was a favorite landmark. Near the outside entrance, a large round tank was a popular spot where folks gathered to watch the harbor seals.

One day after celebrating my son's birthday at a restaurant, he suggested visiting the seals on the way home. When we arrived, three silky coated harbor seals were swimming in tandem round and round the circular tank. Making the turn on the bend, they swam right by us underwater, doing an animated flip to swim upside down, not losing any speed. Seals are symbolic of active imagination, creativity, and lucid dreaming, so maybe their speckled plump gray bodies were in the round pool, but their playful spirit was swimming at sea.

With a fixed smile, sleek, and in control, they rolled and twisted acrobatically round the tank. Every time they swam by us, we sent them love with our hands pressed on the glass.

After five minutes or so, one seal popped his head out of the water. His big eyes never blinking held our gaze.

"I LOVE YOU!" Elliot shouted, pointing at the seal, and he began playing a game, bobbing his head to the right.

Such a public display of affection was a little embarrassing. But, to my surprise, craning his sleek neck, the seal began to play along.

"I love you!" my husband said, again, bobbing his head in the other direction.

I was thankful not too many people were around.

But to our surprise, the seal was game and began mirroring Elliot.

"I love you!" Elliot shouted, bobbing to the right.

The playful seal was enjoying the fun.

"I love you!" Elliot shifted to the left side.

Swaying side to side, this unlikely pair played the "I Love You!" game.

Before long, a whole group of school kids showed up. In no time, a gleeful chorus was now cheering, "I Love You!" bobbing their heads in synch with Elliot and the playful seal. Their joy was contagious. I found myself joining in the fun.

The teacher stood by amazed. The kids got quite an education on love that afternoon, and so did my son and I. The lesson: See all life with love, and don't be afraid to express it!

~The Art of Patience~

*The amen of nature is always
a flower.*
--OLIVER WENDELL HOLMES

After praying at bedtime about a longstanding motherly concern, I opened my eyes. My attention focused on a houseplant from a friend who had moved away the previous year and given us her Schefflera. From across the room, I could see something unusual was happening in that plastic pot. It looked like a flower was ready to blossom.

I got out of bed to investigate and discovered a little miracle, a flower bud. In that moment, it seemed to be the answer to my prayer, and I smiled at the timing.

A perfect message to be patient and know that everything blossoms on time. The impatien volunteer must have been seeded by the wind over the summer when the planter was out in the meditation garden. Pink impatiens bloomed under the old apple tree during the hot season.

In the fall, when the houseplant was moved inside, little did I know of the hidden gift waiting to bloom just when I needed it most.

I thanked the Angels for bringing the flower to my attention.

The next morning, I woke up to find that tight little bud had unfolded. A dainty pink impatien was blooming in the planter beside the tall houseplant.

Wow. Lots of unseen energy had been in the works beneath the soil. So, it may appear as if nothing is happening, but how can we judge what we cannot see, the inner workings that are developing? A good lesson on who can really judge the inner growth of the soul?

Pink is the color of divine love and later I learned that an impatien represents motherly love. How perfect is that?

~A Songbird at Night~

Hope is the thing with feathers
that perches in the soul,
And sings the tune without the words.
And never stops at all.
--EMILY DICKINSON

Sometimes at night, problems can loom much larger than they appear in the light of day, but a song in the dark can help awaken one to the truth. It happened to me.

Lying awake, listening to the quiet patter of rain on the cottage roof, my worry thoughts were interrupted by the sweet song of a bird. *How could she sing in the dark, much less the rain?* I wondered. Sheepishly, I listened from my warm dry bed. If she could sing in her circumstances, why shouldn't I?

I thanked her for a humbling lesson in gratitude for all the blessings I already had received: a roof over my head, free from hunger, and knowing the angels are surrounding me.

Singing can uplift a bad mood, raising it above the clouds of doom where the sun still shines. When problems are mounting, singing is a positive way to express gratitude, indicating all is well with your soul, if not your circumstances. A song is a testimony of trusting that God is All goodness. Wonderful things are happening…because God is wonderful. Whatever is going on brings a gift of more light if I can see it as a lesson to help me grow rather than a punishment. What do I need to learn from this? That is the question most needed.

Several weeks after the songbird called out in the rainy night, another melody came to me in the middle of my sleep. This one I heard in my dream just as I was waking up. The cheerful tune was somewhat familiar although I couldn't name it. Humming it to my sleeping husband, a songwriter, he couldn't place it either. The next day, an "angel" thought whispered that it was from the old Shirley

Temple movie, *Heidi*.

A short time later, the video turned up at a local thrift store. My dream song had indeed been *Heidi's Song*. The orphan had hummed it when she first went to live with her gruff grandfather, a recluse in the Swiss Alps. Rather than let his rude manners spoil her cheerful nature, she happily went about her chores, singing that tune. LaLaLaLaLa lalalala. It was contagious, because soon Grandfather began humming that happy song too.

For the next several weeks, *Heidi's Song* was a hit in my mind. Whenever I was tempted to react, that little ditty would pop up and so would my mood. Things improved and so did I.

~The Mother Mud Dauber~

*...even the insects on my path
are not loafers but have
their special errands.*
--HENRY DAVID THOREAU

On a cool summer day while relaxing under the apple tree something strange caught my eye. A clay-like tunnel had formed on the concrete birdbath. The natural design blended in so well with the butterfly imprint on the pedestal that I wondered how it got there.

Soon, the mystery was solved when I saw a black and bluish winged insect land on the birdbath and crawl into the long clay tunnel. I recognized from childhood that this wasp-like insect was a mud dauber. I fondly remembered their smooth white clumps on the rafters in our old rundown playhouse on the farm. Mud daubers were non-aggressive and stayed focused on building, although their nests were nothing like this masterpiece on the birdbath.

Soon, the little mud dauber crawled out of the tunnel and flew away. Before long, she returned to her nest only to fly away again a short time later. Watching her go about her business, I marveled at how this tiny blue winged one could find her way around our big universe. How did she know where to go to get her supplies and return home?

Fascinated, I witnessed her tireless routine for quite some time, admiring the deliberateness of her activity. With such a display of nature in front of me, I recognized that she must be a messenger.

A search on the web revealed more of the mystery. The mud dauber is the original apartment builder. Not living in a hive with others, she prefers the solitary life and only lays one larvae in her nest. Then, she goes about gathering spiders and insects to attach them to the larvae inside her nest.

So, all those trips to and from were to the "grocery store", bringing food to feed the larvae until it has grown to an adult. Then it can take care of its own needs when it emerges in the spring.

From the size of her "condo", this mud dauber must have been expecting a big heir next spring. When her work is done, she would seal up the opening, her life's mission complete. It would be up to the next generation to repeat the cycle of life.

I found some fascinating information on mud daubers written by George D. Shafer in 1949. After years of study, he discovered that the female mud dauber has a nervous system that enables her to remember, to learn, and to show individuality. Shafer, too, had an affinity for the mud dauber wasp.

A short time later while feeding the birds in the meditation garden, I was surprised to find another "condo" next to the original one!

Twins!

Nature is abundant.

I am learning that out of nowhere, something can suddenly appear to change our view of life. Take a lesson from the mud dauber mother: preserve the future by preparing for new life in the present.

~A New Vision~

Behind the soulfulness of pure saturated light and color,
as best seen in the myriad flowered faces of Nature,
is the beautiful face of God
smiling down in blessing upon us.
--NARANA

Driving to Sandbridge beach on a summer day, one may catch a touch of Monet's art in nature. This beautiful little inlet overflows with bright yellow lotus petals, like satellite dishes on tall stems that radiate joy and happiness by the pondful!

The lotus, also known as the sea rose, is the official flower of Virginia Beach. It symbolizes purity and divine birth, an opening to greater spiritual awareness. The unfolding petals suggest an expansion of the soul. They bring the message that higher knowledge is available if we choose to be open to it. Lotus alerts us to a newer vision unfolding soon.

In Buddhism, the lotus represents purity of body, speech, and mind, as while rooted in the mud, its flowers bloom on tall stems as if floating above the dirty waters of attachment and desires. Drops of water easily slide off its petals, symbolizing detachment.

I had been meaning to take a photo of the colorful blossoming inlet. One day after a severe thunderstorm, the skies cleared, and I returned with my camera, but to my surprise, the wide open yellow petals had closed up during the storm. I didn't know lotus could protect themselves that way.

The next day, the weather had improved. The sun was out, and the yellow lotus petals were beaming, ready to receive a new vision, and so was I.

~Talking with Flowers~

*I love to think of nature as an unlimited
broadcasting station through which God
speaks to us every hour, if we will only
tune in.*
--GEORGE WASHINGTON CARVER

Some may find it foolish to believe that anyone could communicate with flowers and plants. We may all agree that flowers are powerful messengers as their beauty and fragrance stir our hearts, but flowers also possess a spiritual quality that has rarely been explored. When an understanding is gained that all living things share a common life force that is spiritual, then we can open up to the transcendent essence of flowers as they touch our own inner joy and exquisite nature as one with God.

Maybe you've noticed that when you're ready to go to the next level, the universe will present the guidance in unexpected ways, like that old saying, *When the student is ready, the teacher appears.*

Early one morning, I got up to water the garden and beat the heat. The yellow bearded irises, pink mounds of impatiens, red geraniums and cannas, all seemed thankful for the blessing. I felt the light touch of something on the back of my leg. I turned around. A beautiful iridescent green dragonfly lit above my ankle. Dragonflies are very ancient, and symbolize the power of Light. Their appearance can indicate a need to make a change or gain a new perspective on your life. It can also indicate that you are neglecting your emotions and becoming too logical about things.

The dragonfly did herald in a change of perception that day. Turning the TV on, which I rarely do, I landed on a spiritual talk show discussing a fascinating book, *The Man Who Talks With The Flowers. Loving flowers as I do, I was curious about who had authored such an amazing book. It turned out that Glenn Clark wrote it about his dear friend* Dr. George Washington Carver. I remembered studying Dr. Carver in grade school. A prominent Black botanist and inventor, best known for the many uses he devised for the peanut and the sweet potato. But I was impressed that this scientific genius had a deep heart connection with the flowers.

I received the book as a gift and couldn't wait for it to arrive in the mail.

According to Dr. Carver, nature is so anxious to teach us all. The flowers long to share their secrets, but humans must come from love. There is nothing more powerful than love, the life force which holds the stars in their courses. Dr. Carver explained how love is a magnet that draws all things unto it, even the secret truths hidden in rocks and stones.

His secret of speaking with flowers involved a key with three prongs. The first prong represents LOVE. You must love the flowers and be grateful for their presence. Then, HUMILITY is the second prong. It is important to relax all self-imposed emotions. "To talk with the flowers, one must become as relaxed as the flowers, Dr Carver said, including a quote from the Bible: "They toil not neither do they spin, yet even Solomon in all his glory was not arrayed like one of these."

And the last prong to the key is EXPECTANCY. The kind of expectancy born of faith, like seeing a beautiful sunrise, an awe of what is unfolding touches the soul and is the beginning of true wisdom.

Love

Humility

Expectancy

These three attributes must be our consciousness in the presence of Nature. If one prong is missing, the door to speaking with nature stays closed.

I was thankful to Glenn Clark for writing this powerful little book about the secret of Dr. Carver's power of talking with the flowers. "They are mere doorways for him into the infinite world. They are windows through which he sees the face of God" (Clark).

~Food for Thought~

Surrounding me is all life that God created in His Love.
It calls to me in every heartbeat and in every breath;
in every action and in every thought.
--A COURSE IN MIRACLES

A little gray mouse had been appearing all week by the cottage. She was getting rather plump feeding off the birdseed. Her home was in the green wood shed in the meditation garden. One morning she was especially brave, coming out from the shadows to enjoy the breakfast seed buffet alongside a young red cardinal and a bushy-tailed gray squirrel.

"That would make a great picture," Elliot said, watching them from the window. "They're all different, yet one." He smiled.

Do I really want a picture of a mouse? I wondered. Mice are taboo; even though they are intelligent and a member of the rodent family, a mouse is not like a cute chipmunk or rascally squirrel. A mouse is…well, you know.

But I felt guilty for discriminating against this little creature made by God like all the rest of the animals. The Light of God is within her too. I thought about how human races were persecuted in the past because they came into the world wearing a different "costume" that was a red flag to certain people, causing fear.

I watched the mouse nibble on the seed, not knowing she was perceived by me as different from the others. Her needs were the same: water, food, a haven in the storm. Love.

I tried seeing her with eyes of love. "I love you with the love of the Christ," I said, remembering a spiritual lesson. Still that subtle uneasy feeling in my solar plexus stayed. Maybe it stirred a feeling of not being true to myself, after all I had been tossing seed out in the garden for over a year, catching glimpses of the mouse, now and then. Maybe I wasn't ready to come out with my love for her for fear of being judged.

Suddenly I was reminded of the Disney icon that had been inspired by a mouse in Walt's art studio shed. Imagine, that little rodent introduced the inspiration for the Magic Kingdom just by peeking out, taking a risk, and being who he is. The lovable celebrity still brings joyful fantasy to both children and adults.

I thought about the many expressions that describe a mouse: timid as a mouse, quiet as a mouse— my own traits at times.

So, that little creature of God gave me a lot of food for thought on that particular morning. *Mouse* often teaches us to pay attention to detail, take a closer look. And so I did.

~An Angel in the Family~

A Course in Miracles teaches that every problem comes with a solution. So, when a family of mice began to move into the cottage, Elliot and I asked the Holy Spirit for help. It was a lesson in detachment and forgiveness as these little creatures had shredded my good wool navy coat hanging in the closet by the front door. A little research revealed they were using it to pad their nest.

Shortly after calling on the Holy Spirit, *to let me see peace instead of this,* a solution appeared when a good friend came for a weekend visit. Not knowing about our unwanted guests, her announcement of a housewarming gift was the answer: A kitten to be selected by us at the local animal shelters. The quest began, but it didn't take long. I knew I wanted a female black and white tuxedo like my cats in the past.

That afternoon when I saw Angel peeking out of a soft quilted fabric box, the lid on her head, and a pair of golden eyes and pink nose visible inside her cage, it was love at first sight. In the visitation room, Angel rubbed up against my ankles and licked Elliot's hand.

We both knew she was the one. She seemed to understand me when I told her we would come back for her on Monday after her spaying surgery, so not to worry, she had a good home.

Angel was quiet on the ride home in her blue carrier. I sat beside her in the backseat, talking about her new home on the farm. Stopping at the grocery store, I ran inside to buy the cat food brand she had at the shelter. Imagine my surprise, when I returned to find Elliot in the backseat comforting Angel.

Everything went well that evening until bedtime. We understood that night why she had been called Bumble Bee at the Shelter. She bolted out of her *phonograph collar* and then stepped out of a cloth contraption we had devised to protect her incision. I kept her company in the cozy laundry room, but she was still upset, meowing. I returned to my bed and let her be. In the midst of her constant crying, I pictured her in a bubble of White healing Light. We called on the Holy Spirit and the angels for help in comforting her. With compassion, I brought her to our room, but she kept on crying.

So, back to the laundry room. After a few minutes, I sensed somehow that she was in fear, panicking at being stuck with no food or water.

Again, back to our room with her little bed.

But, she couldn't settle down. An angel thought came: *Just give her a few nuggets and a sip of water.* It was against the rules, but I did.

With that touch of TLC, Angel curled up on my pillow above my head. I could feel her furry body leaning against the top of my head like a winter hat. And that was where she would sleep most nights from then on.

Sometimes things have a strange way of unfolding. In looking back, that lovable cat was the inspiration for writing a photo blog on a cat website. Whenever Angel saw me with my camera, she was ready for action, striking a perfect pose. My favorite, lying on her back with one leg propped up on the refrigerator door. Food was her passion…long before dawn.

She inspired me with her bravery, too. Coming home after

dinner out early one evening, Elliot stopped to get the mail and I hurried to the cottage. Angel was napping on the sofa. As I was walking over to greet her, out of the corner of my eye I saw something.

A black snake stretched from the top step all the way down the staircase to the living room!

Fright and flight kicked in.

I exited so fast, not stopping to see which end was up. That snake was either coming down or going up the steps.

I ran to get Elliot. "A snake's in the house!" I told him. He got the property owner, and the three of us returned to the cottage.

Coming back inside, the staircase was empty. He was gone, but that big snake could be slithering free anywhere in the house.

Then, I noticed Angel, posed like a sentinel by the coat closet door in the living room.

"The snake must be in there!" I said. "Look at Angel."

Before they opened the door, I ran upstairs. Standing on a dining room chair, far from the scene, I waited for them open the closet door.

Elliot called out, "It's okay. There's no snake!"

Feeling safer, I came down and sat with my feet safely up on the sofa to watch what would happen next.

I noticed Angel was still guarding the closet door. An old board was propped up at the back of the closet. Could the snake be hiding behind it?

Our property owner had to empty out my six pairs of dirty garden shoes that now laid in a heap by the front door. I was embarrassed; it looked like a centipede lived here.

With the closet floor cleared, it was time to pull the board away. I held my breath. The landlord's wife had joined me, both of us sitting on the sofa, feet up.

"Here he is!" the landlord said.

Angel had done her job. The snake was coiled behind the shelf board.

Now that we'd found him, I had compassion, not wanting the snake to be harmed, just taken out of the house. I silently asked for a holy relationship with the snake.

Using the long wooden handle of his shovel, the landlord somehow got the snake to wrap itself around it. I was so happy to hear him say, "A garden snake is good for mice and rodents." The excitement had passed and he escorted the clinging snake back to the woods.

I'll admit I was feeling guilty for running out of the cottage and leaving Angel to fend for herself. But that fearless cat knew her dominion and held her position of authority, a lesson I have yet to master.

~A Starry Nudge~

(Hubble Photo)

The final mystery is oneself. When one has
weighed the sun in the balance, and measured
the steps of the moon, and mapped out the
seven heavens star by star, there still remains
oneself. Who can calculate the orbit of his own
soul?
--OSCAR WILDE

Our *Search for God* study group agreed on a discipline to practice for the coming week. Before our feet even touch the floor in the morning, set an intention to be a conduit for the love of God that day. A member shared her favorite Edgar Cayce concept as a companion to the discipline, that being to do today what we know to do, to the best of our ability.

Some phrases stick in my mind like calling cards. "Feet touch the floor" became my steady mantra for that week. Long before sunrise, my feet usually touch the floor in answer to the call of a hungry cat. It happened at 5:14 a.m. that fall morning. Feeling well rested, I remembered the practice as my feet touched the floor. "Let me be a conduit for the love of God today." I prayed.

Stumbling down the hallway in the dark, I accidentally stepped on Angel's tail, but she didn't seem to mind since I was on a mission. Food!   After feeding her, I was nudged to look at the stars from our living room window.

I was not disappointed.

The night sky was bright and clear, sprinkled with a canopy of stars so breathtaking that I wanted to be part of it. Opening the sliding glass door, I stepped out in the cool air as if aboard a ship being navigated through the starry heavens. Taking a seat on the deck, a feeling of connection with the past linked me to the stars as I dreamily searched the vastness as those before me throughout the ages. In the silence, absorbing the grandeur of God, I began humbly praying The Lord's Prayer aloud.

I was thankful to Angel for waking me, and for the nudge to embrace the night sky. My feet had led me to be a conduit for God's love today.

~The Balancing Act~

One day in the cottage while reading in the living room, I heard a strange gasping sound and went to check it out. Coming down the hallway, it got louder. In our bedroom, my eyes traveled up the wall. Above the sliding glass doors to the meditation garden, a visitor perched on the metal curtain rod surprised me.

Chest heaving, emitting his weird gasp, a squirrel stared at me wide-eyed. His gray tail was curled above his head like a bushy feather on a fedora. He looked like an actor caught in the wrong scene of a bad play waiting for his next cue. His eyes begged for mercy. Our cat, Angel, was waiting below having interrupted his feast of birdseed in a bag by the door.

Several weeks before the encounter, I had doled out golden raisins to the squirrels day by day, giving them a treat from an aging jar. It was fun watching them nibble away at this delightful treat.

Evidently the quest of the golden raisins had tempted the squirrel inside the house. Looking up at him, I remembered how in the past, passions had left me in a lurch, too.

"Okay, we've got a problem!" I said to him. "I'll get help."

Ushering the cat out of the room, I shut the bedroom door. I

93

was as afraid of the squirrel as he was of me, or I would have opened the sliding glass doors and let him outside to the meditation garden. After all, he was a regular at the morning birdseed buffet, but his insatiable desire for more worried me.

I called to my husband, "A squirrel's trapped in our bedroom! I'm going around to the back and open the slider. Can you coax him out?"

Armed with a dust mop, Elliot went in.

"Squirrely boy, you can come out now," I called from the safety of the meditation garden.

But he was too afraid.

Elliot quickly ushered him out in a cloud of dust. One final gasp of relief although inaudible was felt in my heart as I watched him scurry safely to freedom.

Hopefully, the little squirrel had learned a lesson about balance. Keep your passions in check. A pile of shucked sunflower seeds were found on the floor by the ransacked birdseed bag that I serve every morning. This was evidence that enough is enough. Balance is needed in both giving and receiving in all that we do.

~The Bee Traveler~

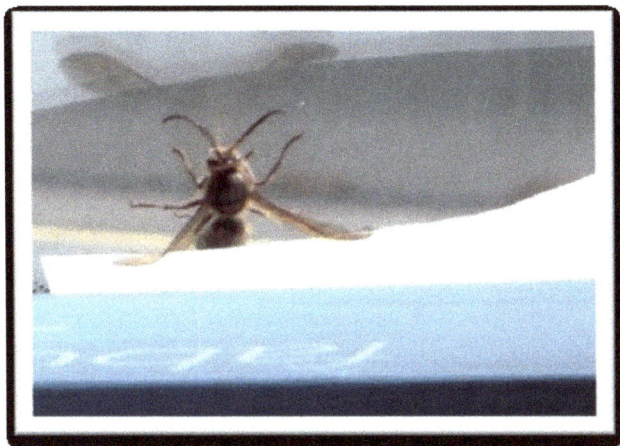

You are as God created you, and so
is every living thing you look upon,
regardless of the images you see.
--A COURSE IN MIRACLES

Elliot and I were trying to practice accepting *what is,* and not reacting if possible. *It is what it is* was our daily mantra. Driving back home on the New Jersey Turnpike, admiring the beautiful shades of autumn, we were enjoying the ride until Elliot looked in the rearview mirror. "There's a bee in the backseat," he said in a calm voice.

"A bee!?" I turned to look. "BEE! You aren't kidding!" A bumblebee as big as my thumb was crawling along the back windshield. Was it one of those big bees from Brazil, I wondered?

The bee looked weary, antennas bent from constantly searching for a way out of a place where he didn't belong. He could see the outside; he just couldn't break through the glass to freedom. Quickly, we rolled down the car windows and found a safe place to pull off on the shoulder of the highway. Elliot hopped out and got in the backseat with the big bee while I bravely did my part, peering in the rear window, calling on the angels for help. I watched Elliot coax the bee with a sheet of paper. "Climb on," he said, "I'll take you to freedom."

With patience, the bee finally crawled onto the paper, but flew off before he was out the door. On the third try, the bee stayed on the paper and was royally escorted outside. As traffic zoomed by, we watched the bee fly upward in an autumn sky free to reach his own destination. "It is what it is," we agreed, accepting the delay as divine order.

The immortal Charlemagne used the bee as a symbol of royalty. There is also an ancient Greek legend that the nine Muses occasionally assumed the form of a bee. The bee is sacred to the goddess Venus, and according to mystics, it is one of several forms of life which came to the earth from the planet Venus millions of years ago. Bees are long time symbols for accomplishing the impossible. The bee is a reminder that no matter how great the dream, fulfillment will come if we keep ourselves busy with divine Love.

~Flowering Power~

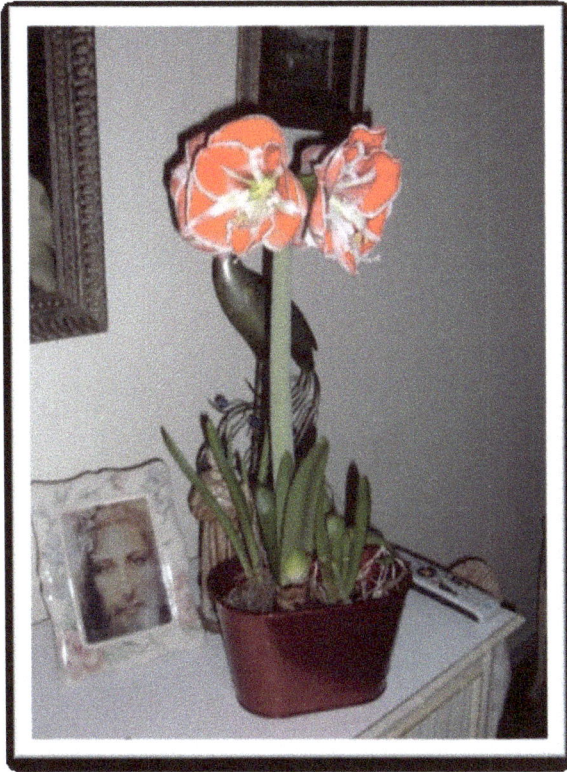

Let every act, every thought be
like a flower opening before God,
and there will be no mistake.
(Talking with Angels)
--GITTA MALLASZ

An early Christmas present arrived in the mail from Hawk, a dear elderly friend. The decorative red planter held a promise of a springtime garden before Christmas. The "crown jewel" was an ugly brown amaryllis bulb that hogged most of the pot. Would anything beautiful come from it? Yet, according to the gift tag photo, a spring garden would bloom bringing joy to the holidays.

I looked forward to watching the flowers peek out from under a blanket of Spanish moss. With a little TLC, soon green sleepy heads poked through to the light. Purple hyacinths, red tulips, white tulips, and white crocus were blooming by Christmas. But the star of the show remained coldly aloof, not responding to the nurturing like the other flowers. There was not even a hint of green emerging from the brown protruding bulb. With such potential, why wasn't it blooming with the others?

I found myself becoming impatient comparing it to other creative projects of mine that had yet to "bloom". Doubt crept in and I thought it was destined to be a no-show, like so many other things that hold great promise but fizzle.

After awhile, I realized my negative thinking was picturing what I didn't want, rather than what I did. Recalling how every flower has an over lighting deva or angel, I asked for help from the Angel of the Amaryllis. Then, I began showering that dormant brown bulb with only loving thoughts, speaking favor over it.

Within a few weeks, a tiny speck of green appeared at the center, so thin, I wondered if it was only my imagination.

With more positive attention showered on the growing bulb, its green stem got wider and higher. It began to shoot up straight and tall like an arrow, taking aim on purpose. At the tip, four tight buds soon emerged.

Remembering that one needs warmth to bloom, I moved the planter to a sunny spot by the window.

A blossom unfolded, opening up like a red and white striped umbrella in springtime. What beauty!

Before long, another blossom opened up, equal in size and beauty to the first, so did the third, followed shortly by the final bloom. Soon, all four blooms, each one facing a cardinal direction: north, south, east, and west, were splendidly blossoming simultaneously.

Scriptures teach, decree a thing and it shall be true to you. By speaking and seeing only the potential of beauty in that drab lifeless bulb, my positive thoughts had also transformed me into a more loving beautiful soul. Each flower must bloom in its own time and in its own way. We can never judge the inward mystery.

~The Power of Prayer~

Sometimes I arrive when God's
ready to have someone
click the shutter.
--ANSEL ADAMS

(Praying Mantis at Tru Blue Gas)

Turning in at a Tru Blue gas station in Seaford, Delaware, on our way home from a road trip to New York, Elliot remarked, "Gas prices are so high." As he pulled up to the pump, the universe echoed his sentiment and seemed unusually playful. At our pump, this praying mantis was on the job, hands praying by the gas nozzle. "Are you praying for cheaper prices, too?" I asked, laughing.

Thanking him for his help, he stayed vigilant as Elliot pumped the gas. His stillness allowed me to take this photo of him praying upside down.

The praying mantis represents power through stillness. Hovering motionless, camouflaged, he blends in waiting for the most opportune time to reach out and grab his reward. If every animal, bird, and insect is on a mission, his message was perhaps to slow down and stay true blue to our Divine Self, go within and remember that your true Source is not dependent on economic shifts. You are a spiritual being dwelling in a physical world.

~A Rabbit on the Path~

The yellow irises had been so plentiful and beautiful. I had brought many from Atlantic Avenue several years prior. They are so giving, quickly multiplying every year. Later, I learned that yellow irises are symbolic of bridging two worlds. Sometimes I would get a little fearful of losing Elliot. He was feeling better, but not quite his usual self. As I laid in bed, I heard: *Trust.* The Angel card TRUST pictures an angel kneeling beside a white unicorn. The unicorn is often a symbol for Christ. I needed the reminder to keep my eyes on Him, and not the problem. Elliot's healing was making me more independent, and helping him to stay grounded in his body.

With the cool sunny weather, I enjoyed the garden. A pair of furry brown rabbits would often visit, romping in the yard. The rascally two would play an amusing game. They would face each other and then spring into action. With powerful hind legs, they took turns leaping up high over their partner's head in a show-down. A real live bunny hop seemed significant. Knowing that rabbit can represent letting go of old fears, maybe this playful pair was teaching a lesson on facing our fears head-on and jumping over them to victory.

Later I came across a dream I recorded in an old journal. It was the story of The Hare and the Cross. A well-known tale in my dream, upon awakening, the story had faded and a search on the web proved fruitless.

One morning while watching the birds and squirrels feed on seed in the garden, suddenly they scattered at once. What had frightened them away?

Curious, I waited, expecting a large predator, but it was only a hungry little rabbit that came out from behind the bushes. I watched her sniff the sunflower seeds in the tray, knowing that to see a rabbit on the garden path was a significant message.

Rabbits are most visible at dawn or dusk, times associated with the Faerie realm. Sometimes a rabbit may appear when we need to do more planning and not end up boxing ourselves in a corner. A rabbit is known for speed, shifting gears from freeze frame to high speed in record time.

To my delight, this gentle creature hopped toward the back steps where I stood looking out from the bedroom glass slider. Motionless, I watched her nibble blades of grass in the morning sunlight that reflected in her big brown eyes. In that moment of trust, an invisible thread seemed to bond us. No longer afraid, she was free, no longer hiding in the shadows. Her bold move was a message to stop my own fearful thoughts and be free.

Silently, I thanked her for the visit and then she turned and hopped over a mound of pink impatiens and scampered back to the woods.

Many years later, when I found this poem written by Saint John of the Cross, on the web, I was reminded of my long-forgotten dream about a rabbit and the Cross and the one who paid me a special visit early one morning.

A Rabbit Noticed My Condition

I was sad one day and went for a walk,
I sat in a field.
A rabbit noticed my condition and came near.
It often does not take more than that to help
at times—
to just be close to creatures who
are so full of knowing,
so full of love
that they don't
chat,
they just gaze with
their marvelous understanding.

The Florida Years. . .

~The Little House on Clara~

What attracts us to a place? Sometimes it is hard to say, because mostly a feeling makes it a fit. You just know that you know—and, that's all there is to it.

The first time I saw the 1927 stucco bungalow, Elliot and I were out for a walk while winter vacationing in Florida. The gray stucco, located a few blocks from the beautiful campus of Stetson University, was for sale by H.U.D. I wished we could afford to buy it.

What I loved best was the large shady backyard with old hardwood trees and an 100-year-old camphor tree, its trunk grey and rough like an elephant's hide. Leafy limbs canopied the bungalow roof giving protection from the heat. Camphor is very healing, and the yard had such wonderful energy that I could almost sense the presence of the nature devas and garden angels. It had such potential!

Hurrying to peek in the windows, I saw that the inside of the house was in need of major repairs. Elliot winced at the bright orange and maroon painted walls and the damaged hardwood floors. "Oh, you don't want to live here," he said. But again, I saw potential.

We returned to the backyard for one last look and decided to send up a blessing for the old house. Standing by the camphor tree, we prayed that this run-down house would be blessed with the perfect owner who would love it and fix it up. Whoever lived here would be blessed and enjoy caring for this sweet spot in nature.

Returning to Virginia in the spring, the house on Clara was soon forgotten. In the fall, Elliot wanted to drive back down to Florida and find a permanent place to live. I found it odd...why not return in the winter and find a place then. But he was so certain that we followed his intuition, armed with our list of rental houses from the Internet. A quick drive-by indicated that none of those was a winner.

Somewhat defeated, we decided that perhaps the trip had been about taking a mini-vacation. After lunch, we drove through the neighborhood near where we had spent the previous winter. "Stop the car!" I told Elliot as he drove down one street. The old grey stucco bungalow was now painted a lovely pistachio green. What timing; the house we had prayed for was now available for rent or for sale! The owner came out to see us and we signed a lease that afternoon. It turned out that he had bought the house in June, and completely renovated the kitchen, bathroom, and fixed up the hardwood floors like new.

We moved into our new home in December. Little did we know that our prayers last winter had been for ourselves.

(The backyard after four years of TLC)

~Teach Only Love~

My lesson from A *Course in Miracles* one day focused on Love, how Love is the answer to every problem: "Begin to look on all things with love, appreciation, and open-mindedness."

An intention was set to practice this and I was soon put to the test. But looking with love wasn't my first thought as I confronted a big stray tabby cat that had been coming around, bullying a weak smaller stray also in need of food. That morning, I lost my patience as I watched the big raccoon tailed cat scare off the skinny little stray feeding from the bowl. In anger, I stormed out of the house and took the food away, fuming. I don't like that bully, I told myself. I want him off the property.

I came inside the house, feeling out of sorts. So much for my *Miracles* lesson.

A sudden impulse made me look out the large dining room window by the driveway. At that moment, the "bully" cat was walking by. Sensing my presence, he looked up at the window.

I stared down at him in anger, but then, suddenly, I was reminded of my spiritual lesson, *Focus on love, look at all things lovingly.* I began trying to send him thoughts of love and kindness. It only took a little willingness before a wonderful thing happened. That ornery striped cat stared up at the window, his clear amber eyes glowing bright as he looked at me. Our eyes met; I continued sending him love thoughts.

To my surprise, he sat down as if basking in the loving energy and kept on staring at me, bright-eyed. Something special was happening between us in that moment. Our eyes seemed to lock in a gaze of divine love, a holy encounter. I felt my heart softening and my vision shifting into a special place that goes beyond words, a sweet space of peace and serenity. Afterwards, I went about my business...and so did he, but I knew we were both better because of that extraordinary exchange.

What started out as an annoying problem became a gift of love. I was so grateful for the experience. That big feral cat became a loving member of our family. We named him Theo. He had taught me to see clearly how my judgments color my world.

Sweeping the patio one morning, I discovered a large pizza crust under the patio table. "Manna," I laughed, wondering where it came from. We hadn't been eating pizza recently. How did it make its way into our fenced yard?

Later, I discovered the breadwinner had been Theo, that big stray love cat was bringing gifts in gratitude for feeding him. The next morning, while sweeping, I found a sub roll under that same chair. More manna, I thought, smiling.

In your giving is your receiving, so give only love.

~Dancing Feathers~

I am like a feather carried on
the breath of God blown
which way he pleases.
--HILDEGARD BINGEN

One morning instead of eating our usual bowl of oatmeal, we grabbed some muffins and hurried to Pine Lake by the Chapel of Divine Mercy. It was a favorite bird watching spot in nature, and this time I had brought along my camera. Sitting in the car facing the water, I thought I saw a white feather floating in the lake off in the distance. It seemed unlikely, yet a feather is a sign from the angels. I watched it bob along in the ripples while eating my muffin. "What's that out in the water?" I asked Elliot finally, not trusting my own eyes.

"Looks like a feather," he said.

"I thought so!" I hopped out of the car. With the camera's zoom, I could clearly see not one feather, but two white feathers! They had crossed paths, forming the letter "X", a union of opposites, male/female or heaven/earth, a balance of polarities.

I kept snapping away, asking the angels for help as I tried to focus on the elusive pair dancing on the sunlit ripples.

"Now, they're in union, riding the current as one." I told Elliot.

"Like you and me," he laughed, watching the "X" feathers navigate through the waters of life.

A trio of sand hill cranes landed beside me. That would have made a nice shot, too, but it was too late. I wanted a photo of the feathers for my nature angel blog.

We laughed hearing a bell ring. A duck had flown up on the bench, shaking the wind chimes. Between the feathers and the bell, no doubt an angel must be getting her wings.

At home, uploading the pictures, the first photo was the only good shot. A search on the symbolism of white feathers revealed more meaning. Feathers represent higher thoughts and white is purity. In dreams, white feathers indicate innocence or a fresh start in a spiritual sense. It turns out that 'X' represents the cross and Christ. It is also a symbol for change or transformation. The letter 'X' represents the Roman numeral ten. In the Hebrew alphabet, a yud is number 10 which means manifestation, as each letter in Hebrew is comprised of yuds.

Looking at the photo, I realized the two white feathers were a reminder to keep thoughts on wings of divine Love as we ride the currents of life. As above so below.

~Who, Who, Who?~

It was dusk when my husband and I returned home from a long trip. I grabbed the phone to make a call from my desk. I was amazed to see a large bird land on the low branch of the camphor tree outside my window. His big eyes stared into my den and we sized each other up for several moments before I hurried to get my camera while he patiently waited for my return. With the zoom lens, I was delighted to see what looked like a large cat with wings perched on the branch. A barred owl!

His appearance was so deliberate that I knew it was a message from the angels. In *Animal-Speak,* Ted Andrews writes: "The owl is a symbol of the feminine, the moon, and the night. I smiled reading it has been called a cat with wings! The owl has great vision and hearing that helps it to hunt in the dark.

The barred owl is the champion vocalist among owls. The barred owl has a benign nature, and this is what is most outstanding about it. It is a great actor and can put on quite a show. Many believe its vocal performances are designed to put other animals and people off. It reflects the ability of this owl to teach us how to use the voice for greater effects."

As I watched him fly away, he hooted Who… Who…Who?

"You. You. You!" I smiled, thankful for the voice lesson.

~Tests of Patience~

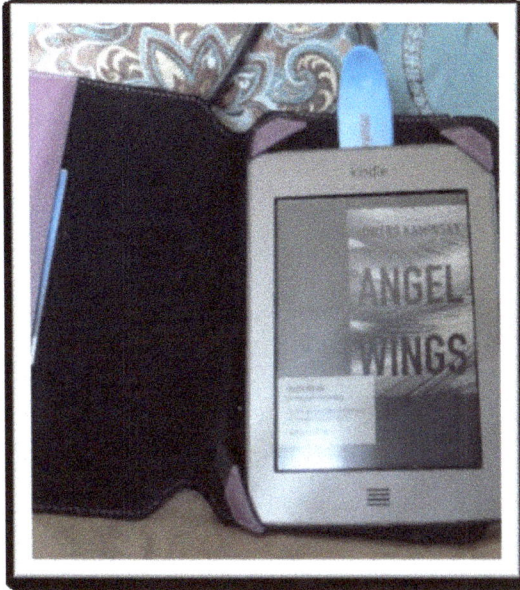

Whenever you are not wholly joyous,
it is because you have reacted with a
lack of love to one of God's creations.
--A COURSE IN MIRACLES

Before dawn, I woke up to the distinct and annoying hum of a tiny mosquito by my ear. Not wanting to disturb my peaceful state of mind, I tried to think of the sound as a merry tune of love. If God is All in all, even a tiny mosquito must share in this substance of Life. I nodded off again, enjoying a little more sleep…until my troublesome troubadour did another "fly by." This time, I swatted the air, and pulled the covers over my head, not having as much patience.

Lying there, I thought about the power of that tiny insect. Compared to me, he was way, way out of his league. Yet I let this little "thing" disturb my peace. That pest is a lot like my ego, circling my head with menacing thoughts, trying to challenge my true identity as a Child of God, a spiritual being made in God's image and likeness.

I got out of bed determined to watch my thoughts, to banish error like an outlaw and arrest any disturbing thoughts before they gained entry at the doorway of my mind.

It wasn't long before I was put to the test. As I began my morning meditation, my next-door neighbor's stereo blasted. "Riders in the Storm" rattled the windows in my den. Halfway smiling, I went with *what is*, and made a decision to be happy in God. External conditions had no power over me. Happiness is an inside job. My meditation went smoothly.

The morning went well until my cat Angel jumped up on my laptop blocking my view. Stubbornly, she refused to budge. A few stern words and she defiantly leaped up on the file cabinet knocking my Kindle on the floor. I lost my peace and a streak of black and white fur vanished down the hallway.

Nervously I opened the Kindle; I was afraid it would be broken. Imagine my surprise to see a book ad light up the screen: *ANGEL WINGS, a mystery*.

I burst out laughing. What timing!

Instead of being angry with Angel, I was grateful for an important lesson. All events are helpful except in the ego's judgment. Just for fun, later I checked my Kindle, curious about the timing of *Angel Wings*.

The ad promo had changed.

So, my cat Angel's timing was perfect. The title *Angel Wings* was the message just for me. Angel cat had taught me to practice love and patience. I'm still working on getting my own angel wings.

~The Rescue Duck~

*The mystery of life is not a problem to
be solved. It is a reality to be experienced.*
--AART VAN DER LEEUW

We had gone again to Pine Lake, a haven for ducks, cormorants, and sand hill cranes, a favorite place to bird watch. One evening a pair of sand hill cranes put on a show. With wings opened wide, facing each other like two hefty ballerinas, they gracefully bounced up and down in a mating dance.

A young woman walked by toting a pet carrier. "Are you releasing a rescue?" I asked.

She sadly shook her head, looking down at a small brown duck by her side. "I'm trying, but she's not ready."

"It's wonderful how you take care of the birds," I said, watching her toss seeds on the ground.

She laughed, shaking her head. "I never liked anything with a beak before."

Her voice got quiet. "Then, three weeks ago, *she* showed up at my door with a gunshot wound."

I looked down at the reddish beak and shiny brown eyes.
"I rushed her to the vet, and we have bonded ever since," the woman told me. "She's been healing my heart as I've been tending to her."

"What's her name?" I asked.

"Dale." She smiled. "We named her that because we weren't sure if she's male or female."

I looked at Dale, now the picture of health, as she waddled close to her guardian.

I watched the two of them do their own dance. The angel woman tried to coax Dale back into the pet carrier to take her home. Only Dale was having a hard time making up her mind. She waddled toward the carrier door, and then waddled off again.

"She's teaching me patience," the woman said, smiling.

Watching them, I wanted to help. Silently, I called on the angels, expecting Dale to be quickly shepherded into the pet carrier.

But, the dance continued—baiting with food— a bowl of water.

I remembered Dale is always God's perfect idea, in her perfect place as a perfect thought in Divine Mind. Regardless of appearance, that truth is changeless.

"Maybe she doesn't want to come with me," the woman said, with a change of heart. "Dale was attacked by a crane near my house. I just brought her from the vet's. They told me not to bring her back home because the crane would get her again." She wiped her teary eyes.

"You did your part." I gave her a hug. "You were an angel when she needed you."

Elliot asked, "What was your intention when you came here?"

"I wanted to release her."

As if on cue, Dale flew up on a tree.

"Maybe that's her way of telling you that she doesn't want to go back," I said.

With a hint of relief, the woman smiled. "I've been following signs. I was planning to drive her to a place eight hours away, but then I learned of this wonderful lake from a woman at the vet's. So, here I am."

We looked at Dale in the tree.

"You've done everything you could," I said. "The same protection that led her safely to you has guided you here. I think you can go, knowing you've helped her."

She nodded, wiping her eyes as she headed to her car. I followed her carrying the empty pet carrier. As she opened the trunk, a distinct sound of wings flapping had us look up.

Dale had landed on the church roof.

"Maybe she's sending you a message," I said, seeing the little duck on the cross. "She wants you to remember her here."

Looking up at her feathery friend, the woman said again, "I've been following signs."

118

"The world's a better place because of you," I said. "Thank you for caring."

Tears were falling from my eyes as I watched her drive away. I wondered, *who had rescued whom?*

People with duck energy often feel uncomfortable with most people in their life. Duck teaches how to find comfort in your own element and with those of like mind and spirit.

~The Daring Jay~

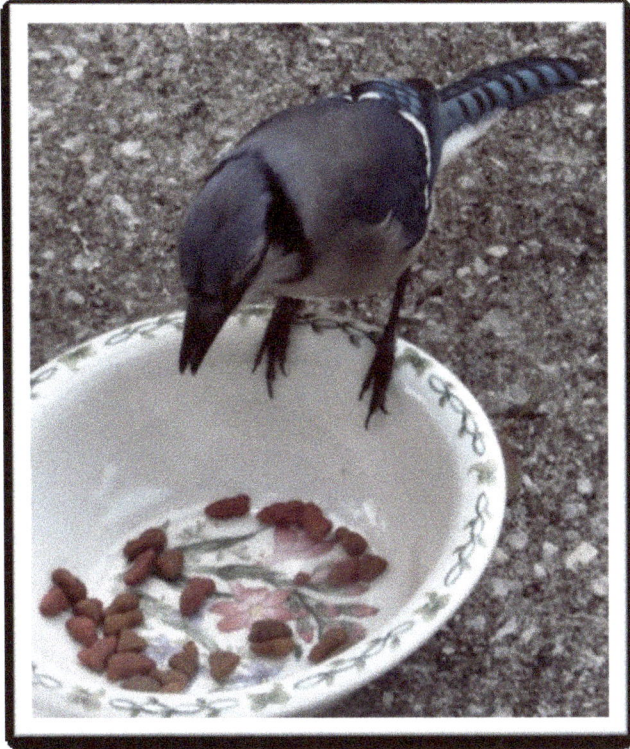

All things work together for good.
There are no exceptions
except in the ego's judgment.
--A COURSE IN MIRACLES

One morning while enjoying the serenity of nature, I was amused to watch a daring blue jay sweep down from the camphor tree and fly real low by the back stoop. What an aggressive move with two stray cats asleep beside me on the patio. Why such a big risk? I wondered.

The answer came a moment later when the same feisty jay swooped down low again—only this time he grabbed a nugget from the cats' bowl, without even landing. A perfect fly-by. I laughed at a bird eating cat food, although, it did seem like an act of oneness. Food is food when you're hungry.

We had stopped feeding the birds when these stray cats adopted us and our yard as their home. Tree climbing felines, they had their own taste, and so to protect our feathered friends, the bird feeder stayed empty.

Within minutes, that persistent jay came back. He landed near the bowl and looked around, about to take a peck. Both cats woke up, and he escaped nugget-free. Maybe his marauding was the cats' karma. They had stopped his birdseed.

I later learned that blue jays are fearless, but also resourceful. They are good at adapting to their surroundings, which this one was teaching well.

I also learned that when a blue jay appears, there will be opportunities to develop your innate potential. The blue jay signals an awakening of great talent. But beware not to misuse the power, and assure power is not misused against you. A wise decision benefits all and does not take advantage or harm anyone.

By proper use of choices, new opportunities will open up. Tapping into your deepest levels, many buried emotions will be brought up, making it hard to choose wisely, but impatience or emotions must not wield in the decision-making.

The blue crest of the jay means a crown of mastership. You need integrity and responsibility to develop the physical and the spiritual. The jay, like all birds, helps navigate between earth and heaven. So don't scatter your energies by dabbling rather than becoming masterful. It takes great concentration to succeed.

That daring blue jay's message: Let go of control, relax, and let nature take its course. Put the birdseed in the feeder. Hang it from the tree. And let everything be as it is. As I learned that day, sometimes my best attempt to control circumstances could do more harm than good, making a risky business.

~Move It!~

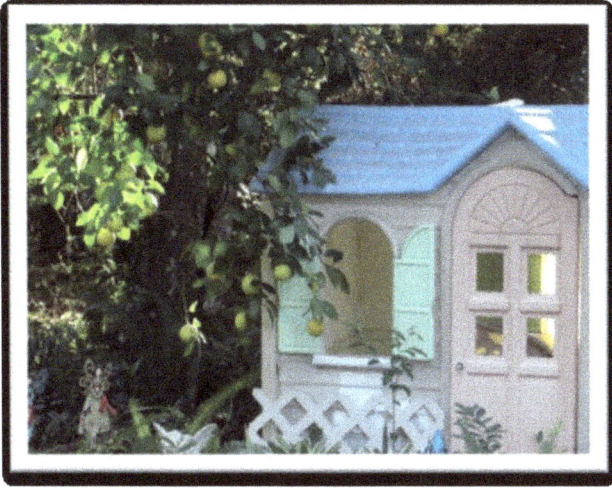

Man's mind is a partner with nature.
--JULIAN HUXLEY

In warm winter weather, I enjoy sitting on the patio with a view of the backyard. In such stillness, I get my best inspiration for working in the garden. A child's playhouse, a rescue from trash, had become a useful shed for housing my garden supplies. The sunray design on the little pink front door inspired the name, Sunshine Cottage.

Relaxing one afternoon, an idea came that involved a lot of work. It was a low energy day, and I wanted to just *be* and not *do* for a change. The inspiration had come to move the Sunshine Cottage further back by the fence under the orange tree. Not wanting to empty the shed, rake the new area, move the shed, and then put everything away again, I ignored the guidance.

The longer I sat on the patio, the more insistent the idea became. Move the playhouse. MOVE IT!

So insistent was the message that finally I gave in and got busy. Working gave me more energy as I not only moved the playhouse, but also made a fairy ring with a border of old bricks. Wild lantana and bromeliads were planted inside the Ring. Theo, our stray love cat, stretched out, watching me work.

When finished, I moved a retro metal lawn chair over by the Sunshine Cottage to sit under the orange tree. It must have been a good idea because Theo curled up under my chair. I thanked the nature devas and the Angel of the Garden for creating sacred space, a healing place to sit in the now, in the serenity of the garden.

This peaceful thought was disturbed by a strong gust of wind from out of nowhere. A bushy camphor twig blew off the tree, hitting the patio where I sat earlier.

A loud crack from a limb was followed by a loud THUD. An 8-foot heavy limb had fallen from the camphor tree. But it came to rest across the arms of my patio chair. I was glad I obeyed and had moved.

Looking up from the safety of my new seat, a shaft of sunlight was shining through the leafy orange tree. "Thank you, God." All my steps had been guided by His angels. "Please, help me listen and be more obedient."

Later, I learned that an orange tree's fragrance and energy are a cleanser for dealing with emotions. The orange tree can help in gently releasing emotional trauma and let go of our fears.

~The Angel of Responsibility~

I randomly picked the Angel of Responsibility card as my angel for the day. A sudden heaviness weighed on me as if I hadn't taken care of something important. But then I remembered another definition of the word: *the ability to respond.*

My *Sayings from A Course in Miracles* card was a good companion for the Angel of Responsibility:

> *Your holy mind establishes*
> *everything that happens to you.*
> *Every response you make to*
> *everything you perceive is*
> *up to you, because your mind*
> *determines your perception of it.*

I read the paragraph referenced in *A Course in Miracles,* and it had the word *responsibility.* It was important to pay attention:

> *Nothing beyond yourself can make you fearful or loving, because nothing is beyond you. Time and eternity are both in your mind and will conflict until you perceive time solely*

as a means to regain eternity. You cannot do this as long as you believe that anything happening to you is caused by factors outside yourself. You must learn that time is solely at your disposal, and that nothing in the world can take this responsibility from you.

(A COURSE IN MIRACLES, Chapter 10)

The word *Responsibility* came up again a few days later in a most unusual way. Angel, my cat, was lounging on top of the new copier/printer by my desk. I was writing on the computer when the machine hummed. Somehow Angel had hit a button.

A photo copy of the *Angel of Responsibility* card popped into the paper tray! Angel was truly a copycat. The Angel of Responsibility had been overlooked by me when the system didn't work a few days before while I was trying to scan the card.

ANGEL OF RESPONSIBILITY. I put it on my desk in plain view as a reminder: *ability to respond.* A major move was coming up for my 94-year old Mom who was leaving her retirement community to be closer to our family. I would soon be flying to Virginia to pack up her apartment. Nervous about flying alone, I worried about the responsibility of the move.

My flight went smoothly, and the cab driver took a detour through Old Town Alexandria where I revisited memories of growing up in the city where I was born. Mom was excited about the move to Florida. The boxes were soon packed and ready to go, but the truck driver was over three hours late that Saturday. Something was wrong.

A satellite trucking company finally arrived with a new contract and no guaranteed delivery date. It was heading for a central hub in New York to unpack Mom's belongings and reload them on a large semi-truck bound for Florida. Bad news. The Angel of Responsibility guided, and we sent the driver away, hoping for a resolution with the original company on Monday morning.

A move can be stressful at any age, but Mom made the best of it while we waited for an answer. Sunday morning, we happened to turn on TV in time to catch Dr. Charles Stanley talk on overcoming anxiety. It seemed his message was meant for Mom and me. God doesn't want you living with anxiety, he said. Sometimes it is warranted, but it's not meant to be a daily way of life. Scripture states time and again to not be anxious. Dr. Stanley recommended that we surrender the problem to God by expressing thankfulness for who God *is*, and who we are *in* Him. Remember all the ways He has come through for you in the past. Then, open your hands and give the problem to Him, whatever it is. Then let Him give you His peace in exchange for it. When this is done in earnest, a buffer of peace will enfold you that transcends human understanding.

That night before going to bed, I got down on my knees and turned the move over to God—thanking Him for all the ways he had come through for me before. When I got back into bed, a peacefulness settled over me, and I slept. I had turned everything over to Him: our expenses (non-refundable airline tickets, extra night's lodging at Mom's retirement complex), and her empty apartment packed and ready to go with no idea when, or how, it would happen. 18-wheelers were too large to enter the entrance gate at her new residence, but it was now God's problem, and surprisingly I had peace.

On Monday morning, my peace stayed with me even though the original moving company didn't return my calls. Guidance came to search the yellow pages for a new mover. I asked the Holy Spirit for help in finding the right one

The owner of Sterling Van Lines answered the phone and listened to our problem. Then, he asked my Mother's name.

"Mary Luckie," I said, with a chuckle.

"Well, she may not have been lucky on Saturday, but the Lord *is* at work in her life," he said.

"AMEN." I said, feeling lighter. Arrangements were made for an expedite by his company the next morning. On schedule, they arrived, her belongings were packed and on their way. Mom and I would fly to Florida on Tuesday.

That last morning at The Fairfax, I was awakened before sunrise by a joyful loud call of Canadian geese. Flying over the roof, the flock's joyful honking made me laugh as they splashed down in the lake outside our bedroom window. I love geese, knowing they represent heeding the call to the quest. Listening, it may have been my imagination, but their honking sounded like the name of Mom's new retirement home in Florida, The Cloisters.

CLAC—CLAC—CLAC—CLOIS—STERS...

CLA—CLAC—CLAC—CLOIS—STERS

Joy was in the air! The past 17 years at The Fairfax, the Canadian geese had Mom spending hours bird watching from her 4th floor apartment view of the lake.

Mom and I would be flying out that morning. I was thankful that the Angel of Responsibility had given me the right clue on moving day. A heavy winter storm had hit up north, so no telling when Mom's shipment would have arrived via snowy New York City.

A short time later, Mom was settling in to her new apartment when a sweet surprise turned up while shopping. A flock of Canadian geese had followed her to Florida, making their way to her living room in Dan Griffith's beautiful painting. In his work of art, the flock had flown safely through a bank of dark storm clouds—a portal of light had opened up to reveal the green grass of home below. They had safely made it, and so had we. Interesting to note, her apartment number in Florida was the same as it had been in Virginia, No. 420, but that's another angel story.

Canadian geese are compassionate birds. They never leave behind an ill or wounded fellow bird. They also make good leaders as they take turns knowing when to lead, and when to follow, alternating roles. I was thankful to have turned the lead over to the Holy Spirit.

~Buddy, The Horse Healer~

Everything you teach you are learning.
Teach only love, and learn that
love is yours and you are love.
--A COURSE IN MIRACLES

While ordering lunch at the Creative Artists' Cafe in Lake Helen, Florida, I looked up from my menu in time to see an unusual customer. A striking horse was looking to be served. He had poked his brown head inside the Takeout Window. Mr. Ed, the 60's talking horse TV show brought back childhood memories. Playfully, I wondered what this tall dark stranger had ordered. When a horse shows up, it may bring a lesson to ride in new directions, and to discover your own freedom and power. My horse's appearance seemed to be saying, "Put in your order, and it will be served to you."

When I looked again, he was gone.

"Did I see a horse at the takeout window?" I asked our server.

"Oh, that's Buddy." She laughed. "He belongs to the manager of the Cafe. He loves to come to the window for his peppermints."

A real horse at a restaurant was most unusual. Lake Helen is horse country, but this was a first.

I have always been fearful of horses. They are so big. And, the thought of putting my hand near a horse's mouth.... But, I had been trying to recapture the innocence and joy of a child, so after lunch, I went outside to meet Buddy.

His dark brown eyes were understanding as I nervously reached up and held out my hand. SLURP. Buddy gummed my fingers as I talked to him. He wouldn't stop licking my hand—maybe the turkey burger flavor kept him at it.

I found my heart softening as I surrendered, and just let him love me. He leaned his head up against my shirt and tried to nibble it.

"You're so handsome, Buddy," I told him.

It turned out that Regina, the manager, had taken a horseback ride to town. "He picks up the pace when the Cafe comes into sight," she said, smiling. "He heads straight for the carryout window to get his mints."

I told Regina this was the first time I had come close to a horse. She laughed. "He doesn't seem to know the difference. He loves you."

Horse is symbolic of movement and life force. Life is full of wonder and excitement. I walked away wearing a big grin. Thankful to have wisely chosen to move forward in love over fear, I now had a new *Buddy*.

~What Are You Parroting?~

(Parrot Photo from Wikimedia Commons)

Life is full of surprises. I was in for a day of watching my thoughts. On my way to meet a friend for lunch, the annual Arts Festival had Main Street blocked off. The restaurant parking lot was also closed. I was on foot, and began to worry if Joanna would have trouble parking, but I caught myself and decided to thank the angels for guiding her to the perfect spot.

As it turned out, she had arrived before me and arranged for a lovely table outdoors by the manatees waterfall fountain. I could see how things were in divine order. Joanna had found the last parking place in a nearby lot.

As I pulled out my chair to join her, a woman at the table behind me worriedly confided that she was meeting someone for the first time for lunch. They had met on the Internet and he was coming from out of town to meet her face to face. With the Festival in town, where would he park?

Having already experienced an act of divine timing, I told her not to worry, the angels would guide her date to the perfect parking space. She smiled and took my hand, grateful that we both spoke the same language. Before long, he made an appearance.

While Joanna and I enjoyed a good meal in the sunshine, I spotted a shiny penny by the fountain. A sign from the angels not to worry, everything is in divine order. A small lizard, sunning on the railing, scurried away as I retrieved the penny. Detachment is the lesson lizard brings and I would soon be met with a chance to do so.

Passing by a row of tables on our way out, I noticed a man busy texting while dining in the patio area. His partner idly sat across from him at the table. At first glance, I mistook the stately white parrot for a toy bird, but it blinked, and turned its white feathery head toward me. A parrot, dining out was a first for me.

"You're real!" I said with a smile. He even had his own little bowl of water on the table.

Picking up on my interest, the man stopped texting, eager to put on a show. "Do you love me?" He asked the beautiful bird.

On command, the parrot hopped onto his master's hand where he was lifted up and gave him a tender peck on the ear.

His owner again commanded, "Give me a kiss," I watched the obedient parrot cock his feathery head and plant a big smacker right on his master's lips.

This bird was well trained. Joanna and I laughed, but as we were walking away, having said our goodbyes, I was taken aback by the next command. "Now, flick off the nice ladies."

Not sure I'd heard him right, I turned around in time to see that big white parrot raise up one leg and stick up a big black talon at me.

I didn't know… should I laugh or be insulted? But it was such a rare comical sight, far too funny to be insulting. The first time I'd been given the "bird" by a bird. I laughed. "Now, you have to give me a kiss," I playfully told the parrot. But his only response was a blank stare and I moved on.

Curious, I looked up the symbolism. A parrot is known as a record keeper for the thoughts you are parroting to yourself. My ego has a barrage of insults for every occasion.

That brazen parrot also taught me another lesson. When someone behaves rudely, I don't have to take the insult personally. I can laugh it off, and move on without pointing a finger.

In *Angel Messages, The Oracle of the Birds:* "The parrot, with its deafening squawk, rudely awakens us out of our sleep of complacency and spiritual idleness, and urges us to aim for higher things."

Early the next morning, I awakened to an inner voice, "Be still and know that I am God." I thought about that trained parrot who was obedient only to his master. It got me to thinking, what voice do I respond to? The Holy Spirit or my ego?

~A Leaping Lizard!~

When we try to pick out anything in Nature,
we find it hitched to everything else in the universe.
--JOHN MUIR

Lizard is often associated with dreams or dreamtime and brings a lesson in detachment. I was having a problem in separating myself from a controlling difficult relationship when an encounter with a lizard helped me learn to let go.

It's hard to say when I overcame a fear of lizards. At the cottage on the farm, I became familiar with the little blue and yellow striped skinks. Often I would see them basking on a large rock in my flowerbed. I began to see these little creatures as cute and animated, although, the last thing I ever wanted to do was to touch one.

It turned out the three years on the farm in Virginia had been good training for a future move south. Living in Florida, lizards are a natural part of the landscape, posing on garden statues or climbing the warm exterior stucco walls of the house. I found myself becoming rather fond of them—at a distance.

The balance in nature shifted when those two stray tabbies, Theo and Mr. Paws adopted us, and our backyard. We hoped the lizards would be safe since these two cats were now well fed. The garden was to be a peaceful sanctuary for all life.

One afternoon, Mr. Paws caught a small lizard in his mouth and brought it over by my chair on the patio. A most unwelcomed gift, he dropped it by my feet. The lizard froze, playing dead... Mr. Paws waited...until it made another move, before taking another pounce. The game was hard to watch.

Silently, I asked the Holy Spirit and the angels for help. Looking out at the serenity of the garden lovingly co-created with nature, I affirmed, that all of God's creatures move together in harmony.

I knew it was important not to interfere with nature, but still...

Mr. Paws was relentless.

Sitting at the umbrella table, I closed my eyes, affirming harmony, once more. When I looked, the lizard had gone. A puzzled Mr. Paws sniffed around, but he couldn't find his prey.

Something made me look down. That little lizard was clinging to my jeans just below my knee! Looking up at me in terror, I could almost hear his silent, but loud cry, HELP! His tail was gone, but he was alive. There was hope. It would grow back again. But, what a bold move for him to trust me. Why hadn't I jumped up, brushing him off with a scream?

My calm reaction surprised even me. Funny, in that moment, I realized that I *was* the answer to *my* own prayer. Silently, I told him to hang on. Slowly I got up from my chair. I marched across the yard like a stiff legged tin soldier on parade. Reaching the trees, I looked down. My hitchhiker had safely let go somewhere along the way. And, I was free from worry about his fate.

Mr. Paws sniffed the patio, but soon gave up. I must admit when it was all over, I began to cry, not sure why. Maybe my love for that scared little lizard exceeded my fear of him, and in that moment I was transformed. Perfect love had cast out fear.

Lizard teaches to pay attention to your intuition or else you may be swallowed up by something that is unhealthy for you. With a keen sense, lizard can see things that others may miss—hear things that are not being said. To survive, the lizard can detach its own tail and distract its predator so it can escape. The lesson my lizard brought was a need to separate myself or part of myself to achieve the things I need to do. Like my lizard friend taught me, we may need to lose our tail to get ahead.

~The Ark~

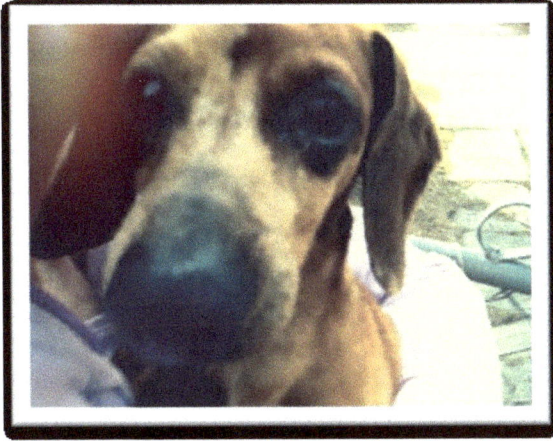

If you put your heart against the earth with me,
in serving every creature,
our Beloved will enter you from our sacred realm
and we will be, we will be, so happy.
--RUMI

What could be causing a traffic jam in front of our house? I watched from the front porch in our new neighborhood. Soon a little brown dachshund, dodging cars, ran into the woods across the street. A blonde in a black sports car tried to take command of her charge, but he was on an adventure, having jumped out the car window.

I watched her speed away, to head him off on the next street, but she returned empty-handed. She spoke to my neighbor across the street who was tinkering with his car. Then, she drove away.

Expecting the little dog to run out of the woods, I waited, asking the angels for help. Before long that short-legged "dash hound" was back in the street. Clapping my hands, I called out, in hopes of corralling him inside our fence. But those stubby legs raced him down the middle of the street. Cars braking—coming and going—it was hard to watch, but I affirmed: *All of God's creations move in perfect harmony.* Now just a brown speck many blocks away, I asked the angels to watch over him and deliver him safely to where he needed to be.

The chase seemed hopeless, but something kept me in pursuit as Elliot rigged up a leash. We were about to jump in our car when a woman drove up in a blue SUV, shouting, "We've got your dog!"

Her young red haired son held the shaking puppy in his arms. An angel assignment, no doubt, with such a speedy delivery. They drove away leaving me with a bundle of quivering love.

The hardest part was over— he was safe. *Thank you, Angels.* I sighed, watching for his owner by the road with him cradled in my arms. With each passing car, my hopes faded. The minutes grew longer. The temperature dropped and the short-haired rescue began to shiver. I left him on the sun porch with Elliot, and waited alone.

Time passed slowly. I decided to name him Indy, short for Indiana Jones, and the Indy-500 race. The speed in which he raced down the road, skillfully dodging oncoming cars and his adventuresome spirit, taking a daring leap from a moving sports car made the name a fit.

It was almost dark when an angel thought suggested introducing myself to my neighbor across the street. Maybe he knew what happened. I was glad I did. Indy's owner had gone to the airport to pick up her husband and would return in two hours. She asked my neighbor, Manny, to keep her dog for pay if he turned up. She would check back later.

Manny came over to meet her dog. He generously donated some dog food for dinner. We all decided Indy should stay at our house since Manny had a dog, and Indy was content where he was.

"You're going to have a house guest tonight," my son told us. "She's not coming back." Our little Angel cat gave me a look like, *You have GOT to be kidding!* Her friendly hiss and his bounding spirit were no match.

How could anyone abandon this precious little canine? I wondered, watching Indy sleep curled up on a soft purple blanket on the wicker loveseat. Late that evening, a last minute trip to the store had Indy set for the night: a leash, collar, and a can of dog food.

Indy slept in my son's room, and Angel cat slept on our bed. The house was quiet and peaceful as I affirmed again: All God's creations are harmonious.

Indy's owner never returned, for some unknown reason, she had abandoned her pet. The next morning, I wrestled with an idea to adopt our little runaway who was just like my childhood dog, Waldo. But it wasn't fair to Angel, who wasn't behaving like one to our guest.

An angel message reminded me of an animal rescue house on Main Street. The Ark, a sanctuary for furry friends answered my call that morning. Indy was in my arms as we entered The Ark. The symbolism wasn't lost on me. A woman greeted us with a warm smile. She lovingly told my little friend, "Just yesterday a lady was in here, looking to adopt a sausage dog. I kept her number." Patting Indy's head, she said, "That woman was a day early, but I have a home for you."

"He's so cute," she added, taking him in her arms. "What's his name?"

"Indy" I said, explaining why, with a tearful goodbye.

"That's a great name," she said, with a smile.

On the drive home, I thought about the people who'd led to Indy's rescue. Each event involved divine timing and teamwork so Indy could make it safely onto the Ark.

~A Lesson in Communication~

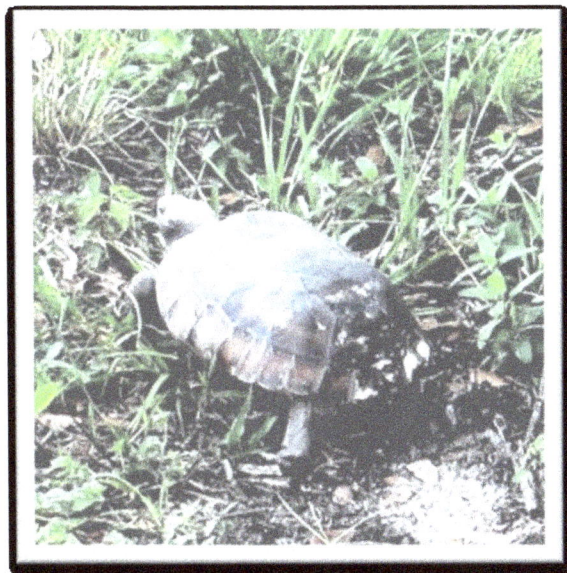

On a beautiful fall day, El and I took a walk through Blue Springs Park in central Florida. Stopping on a lookout deck, we hoped to see the manatees, but the water temperature in the St. Johns River wasn't cold enough for them to swim inland to the Springs. Watching the clear blue waters, a large single fish swam by and Elliot waved.

"Why are you waving to a fish?" I playfully asked. "Do you think he can see you up here on the deck?"

Elliot smiled and assured me that the carp could feel the love vibration. He must have been right—a large school swam over to join in the energy. I did think it a bit much when he then sent love to a smiling gator, but love was in the air.

On our way home from Blue Springs, an opportunity to share love came when a turtle ambled out of the woods towards the busy road. A residential neighborhood on the other side seemed to be his destination. With his home on his back, he could set up housekeeping wherever he liked.

Remembering another time when I hadn't stopped to help, I asked Elliot to pull over. The turtle was heading in the wrong direction. With a stick, I gently prodded the turtle to turn around. As hard headed as his shell, he retreated inside, refusing to listen to reason. "Get a life of your own," his actions told me.

I confess I talked to him about the wisdom of not crossing the road. But he paid me no mine and turned back around toward the traffic again.

"Have it your way," I said, having tried to help him change his way. Now watching my turtle friend lumber over twigs and grass heading for a new adventure, I had to let go. Angels were overseeing him. Snapping a photo, I wished him well. He was on a mission. A young woman driving by saw me take his picture. She stopped with her camera. "See what you can do to keep him safe. He's trying to cross this busy road," I told her.

She nodded with compassion.

As Elliot pulled away, I shrugged, thinking of how letting go happens in degrees, but I'm getting there as fast as a turtle.

A turtle's shell on his back is a symbol of heaven, and the square underside symbolizes the earth. If a turtle appears on your path, expect blessings from both realms.

~The Fan of Creativity~

When an animal makes a spectacle of itself on your path, it is wise to pay attention. Chances are that its behavior at the time you meet, as well as its special characteristics, can offer insight as to what's happening in your inner life. If you are watchful, you may be surprised by the energy exchange it brings your way.

Looking for a possible new place to live, Elliot and I were driving through a residential neighborhood located in nature. We saw an unusual resident out for a stroll. At first glance, the wild peacock appeared to have escaped from a fairy tale. He strutted across a driveway, dragging his long plumage. Standing by a closed garage, he knew where to go for food.

I wanted to take his picture with my cell phone. His backside was dull, not at all photo worthy. Then, in one WHOOSH— his feathers fanned out like an umbrella popping up in one motion. That magnificent rush of energy could have raised the garage door like a genie.

I got out of the car to capture his picture as a neighbor walked by. "Wait a minute, he'll turn and you'll get a better photo." She smiled. "He's a regular. If you lived around here, you could see him all the time."

My own imagination began to fan out from the mundane to the extraordinary, opening wide to experience the rich spontaneity of life. The thought of a beautiful wild peacock living in the woods nearby stirred a sense of wonder. Just then, like a seasoned runway model in a blue-green iridescent gown, he proudly pivoted, coming full circle. His layered feathers like "eyes" send a message to be watchful, and we were getting an eyeful of his beauty.

The couple who feed him returned home.

"He's so beautiful," I said, admiring him as he waited by the garage door.

The husband smiled. "He's just a pretty beggar coming by for something to eat."

"And, he's so fussy," his wife laughed. "He likes this kind of cereal, but not that."

Elliot said, "Well, he certainly likes you."

On our drive home, we admitted that his visit had transformed our world in a strange and exciting way. It turned out that his appearance fanned our creativity as we both worked late into the night on new creative projects.

Peacock symbolizes resurrection and wise vision/watchfulness. In ancient Egypt, it was associated with the all-seeing eye of Horus, the hawk. In Christianity, it is known as a symbol of the death and resurrection of Jesus, and represents immortality. The peacock's call, a screech like laughter, is a reminder not to take things too seriously.

Like attracts like. A closer look revealed the peacock energy already present in our life. My daily peacock journal, a peacock notebook in the car, and a peacock cardholder in our kitchen window. It has *A Course in Miracles* card to help me focus on my rights:

You have the right to all the universe;
to perfect peace, complete deliverance
from all the effects of sin, and to the
life eternal, joyous, and complete in
every way, as God appointed for His
holy Son.
--A COURSE IN MIRACLES

~The Hummingbird~

God is the friend of silence.
See how nature...
Trees, flowers, grass
Grow in silence.
See the stars, the moon and sun
how they move in silence.
The more we receive in silent prayer,
the more we can give in our active life.
We need silence to be able to touch souls.
--UNKNOWN

Our peaceful Saturday afternoon was suddenly interrupted by five jets that emerged flying in low formation over our neighbor's trees. Heading toward our house, the deafening decibels shattered our nerves and rattled the windows. Ducking down on the patio, Elliot and I covered our ears while Theo made a mad dash under the house crawlspace.

Regaining our composure, we wondered where they came from? Military jets from nearby Oceana Air Force Base were the norm while living on the farm at Virginia Beach, but this fly-by was a first here in DeLand.

Grateful for silence, Theo returned from underneath the house.

Soon we became gently aware of another winged one. A delicate ruby throated hummingbird flitted about an orange flowery spike on an aloe vera plant. Nothing can win one's affection as quickly as the rare sight of a hummingbird in the garden. Fascinating to watch, he probed each tender blossom's nectar.

Passing close by, his iridescent feathers reflected the sunlight. What a contrast in our recent experiences, the thunder of jets, and the gentle beauty of a hummingbird darting among the flowers. Although this little flyer didn't have the power to thunder across the skies, he was able to make long journeys from Alaska to Central

America. And, like an ace pilot, the hummingbird can reach high speeds as it takes off. It is skilled at stopping immediately in flight, in flying backward, forward, sideways, or just hovering. This little bird was born to fly and unlike other feathered friends, it cannot walk.

When one appears on your path, it is a symbol of joyfully doing what others may find impossible. The hummingbird is fearless of other birds. Regardless of our circumstances, when a hummingbird shows up he brings the joy of accomplishment.

Later I learned that the aloe vera plant heralds a time to soothe irritations that we are encountering. Our skin is our largest sensory organ and most things we encounter register through our skin. Aloe is healing to skin conditions and the hummingbird had soothed the irritation of the deafening jets that afternoon.

~A Special Valentine~

Put your thoughts to sleep,
do not let them cast a shadow
over the moon of your heart.
Let go of thinking.
--RUMI

I've always had a special fondness for the moon, waking in the night to a soft glow of moonbeams on the pillow. The moon has no light of its own, but reflects the energy from the sun. A favorite quote about the moon comes from that classic movie *It's a Wonderful Life*. George, played by Jimmy Stewart, offers to lasso the moon for his sweetheart Mary, (Donna Reed). Mary tells George, "I'll take it, then what?"

"Well, then you can swallow it, and it'll dissolve, see...and the moonbeams would shoot out of your fingers and your toes and the ends of your hair..."

I love that healing imagery. An experience with the moon especially touched my heart one winter. It happened by chance, but as we know, one thing always leads to another in the realm of giving and receiving.

Mom had called to report a hard freeze was in the forecast for our area. It was almost dark when I hurried out to the garden, arms piled high with blankets and comforters. Theo, our frisky outdoor tabby, playfully circled round my legs as I tried to keep my balance along the garden path. In the cold night air, I quickly made the rounds, tucking in the bromeliads, azaleas, irises, and ferns.

Afterwards, that rascal cat took my work as a blanket invitation to curl up on a soft quilt and settle down for the night. Pausing to watch his gray striped body snuggled up by a tree, I noticed the beautiful moon shining through the treetop. It was so beautiful that I ran for my camera. Gazing up at the bright full moon, the lens magnified until something amazing happened.

The moon grew so magnificently big and full that to my eyes it looked like a cosmic gazing ball. The imprint of leafy branches blended earth and heaven together in a moment of tender embrace. Heavenly light and earthly trees captured a fond memory, as I suddenly remembered that tomorrow was Valentine's Day. Love was in the air that moonlit night warming my heart with a new vision.

~Free Your Spirit~

I was amused by the odd behavior of a cute bird that had been popping up on my path. The first time I saw a cattle egret, he stood like a hood ornament on a parked car in town. Before I could get a picture, he flew away, but I thanked him for the message: "It's time to shift gears from (P)ark to (D)rive. Get moving!"

A few days later, he made another spectacle of himself as he swooped down landing on a tree outside a restaurant in town. Watching us through the window, he brought tidings to my friend's birthday celebration. Soon he flapped his wide white wings and flew above the traffic on Main Street, free to follow his Spirit without limitation.

I wanted a photo of this comical bird, but the opportunity didn't appear until a drive through the country that weekend. What a surprise to find him in a pasture hanging out with an unlikely friend. A horse. They looked so cute together and presented a double meaning:

A cattle egret brings an angel message to break out of 'the herd' and let your Spirit fly free...a wonderful companion for a pent-up horse, don't you think? Horse represents movement. It's time to giddy up!

~The Sacred Tree Speaks~

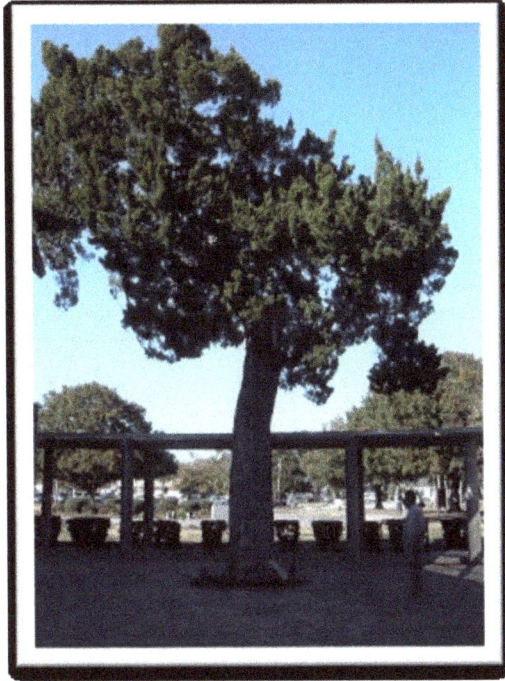

Sometimes being "in the flow" can be deceiving, like not finding a parking spot on a Saturday afternoon in busy historic Saint Augustine, Florida. Driving around an endless maze, we asked the angels for help, but it just wasn't happening. The downtown area was so congested that we decided to skip the adventure and return to our hotel. Other plans were in the works, but on our way out of the historic district, a parking spot on the street had opened up by a large church in a nature setting.

With my camera in hand, we were off exploring. In the courtyard of The Prince of Peace Church, I saw a favored tree standing alone on a large stone patio. From a distance, I took a picture, wondering if it was a cedar of Lebanon.

Elliot walked on ahead to read the plaque by the old tree.

"What does it say?" I asked, coming closer.

"It's a message from the tree," he said.

"The Tree? I laughed. "Are you kidding?" But he was right. I began to read the poem out loud, feeling my eyes mist.

The Sacred Tree

I am a Child of God, just as you.

Behold me! The silent witness,
I have known it all,
Listen to me as I speak
through the wind.

I am a child of God, Just as you.
He sends me water from the clouds.
He sends me light and warmth of
the Sun to nourish me.

It is my responsibility to
provide you with clean air and
shade.
I shelter you and keep you.

Beneath my boughs, deer have grazed,
and Native children played.

Beneath me I have seen the vices of men:
greed, ambition, deceit,
And the virtues of faith, courage,
compassion, heroism,
Even self-sacrifice.

I am a child of God, Just as you.

Learn from those who have gone
before.
Bend, but hold your truths; stay
strong and persevere, as I have.

Come, don't be shy; place your hand
upon me.
I will share my strength with you.
God has given us all many gifts.
Rejoice in them, share them.
I am a child of God, Just as you.
We are all God's children.

Our next trip to Saint Augustine we found another "special tree" on Cordova Street in the historic district. The "Love Tree" is an odd couple, a sable palm tree had grown out of the "heart" of a live oak. For years these two have shared a fond embrace, co-existing in harmony. If they were to be separated, both would surely die, as they are one in union. According to an old legend, if you kiss your beloved under the Love Tree, you'll have an everlasting romance—a real true love's kiss, so we puckered up.

(Love Tree)

~Share the Sunshine~

Make you the world a bit better
or more beautiful because
you have lived in it.
--GRANDMA of EDWARD W. BOK

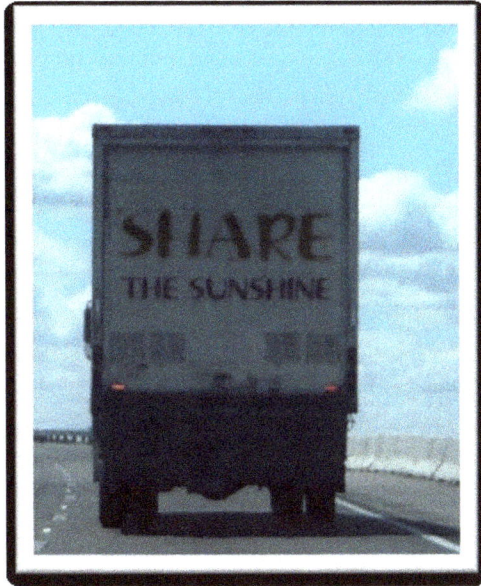

Inspiration came on my husband's birthday to take a spontaneous road trip to Lake Wales, Florida. Birthdays are a time of celebration so we packed up the car and took off for Bok Tower, a 50-acre historical site on central Florida's highest point, known for its beautiful gardens. A singing tower has 60 carillon bells—one weighing almost 12 tons—a perfect place for a musician to spend his birthday.

On the highway, a truck up ahead had a great logo: "Share the Sunshine", something we could all practice more.

Entering Bok Tower gardens, with the windows down, a heavenly scent of orange blossoms filled the air as we drove through acres of orange groves. On a hill in the distance, a 205' tall pink marble Tower resembled a spire from King Arthur's castle.

The area had once been an arid sand hill where Edward W. Bok enjoyed evening walks among the pines to the top of "Iron Mountain". There he was inspired by the beautiful sunsets to preserve the hilltop and create a bird sanctuary—a place of beauty and serenity.

By doing so, this Pulitzer Prize winning author and philanthropist would also fulfill the advice of his Dutch grandmother: "Make you the world a bit better or more beautiful because you have lived in it."

President Calvin Coolidge dedicated the Tower and Sanctuary in 1929. Florida birds: the pelican, the flamingo, the heron, the goose, and the swan were sculpted in a decorative band at the top of the Singing Tower. Eagles were part of the design as the sanctuary is a gift to the nation. The dove, a symbol of Edward Bok's commitment to world peace, can be seen in many styles and material throughout the tower and gardens.

Elliot and I arrived early and had breakfast in the café with a view of the beautiful grounds. Soft instrumental music played while we ate our muffin. The only two early birds in the restaurant, I found a business card tucked inside the napkin holder on our table. *You were created in the image and likeness of God…*

God's business card, it was a reminder of what I had been trying to learn recently. "I am made in the image and likeness of God," I affirmed, smiling at the synchronicity. I wondered if these calling cards were on all the tables. But the angels must have been at work since our table was the one of choice that morning.

Knowing my true identity, life can be experienced as heaven on earth, and what joy to share the sunshine.

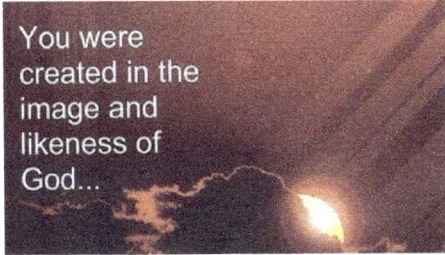

You were created in the image and likeness of God...

~Ladybugs on Parade~

...commune with your own heart upon your bed,
and be still.
--PSALM 4:4

A trip to northern Virginia to see our new granddaughter was bittersweet as it was also the first time "home" since my Mom's passing that summer. We had many fond memories of autumn with Mom in that area. Virginia had been her home before she moved to Florida to be near us.

Without Mom, I was feeling blue, missing her and the times we had shared. Resting on the hotel bed, gazing out of a large picture window, I was enjoying the rich colors of autumn leaves. That's when I spotted a little bug on the inside windowpane. I got up to see what it was.

To my delight, a ladybug had come to visit, a childhood favorite.

I laid back down and watched it crawl around on the windowpane. Since the hotel window was sealed shut, I wondered how it got inside the room. Was she searching for a way out? Before long, many ladybugs had joined in a parade around the autumn window. Curious, I looked for an opening, but it remained a mystery as to how they appeared.

Wanting to help them find their way out, I asked the Holy Spirit for a holy relationship with these busy visitors. Talking to my "lady" friends about the joys of freedom, I encouraged four ladybugs to crawl into an empty drinking glass and covered the lid. Quickly I escorted them into the elevator, down five floors, and out into the sunshine again.

I called out to the last one, "Fly away home!" Her wings snapped open on the tip of my finger and I watched her take flight in the cool autumn air.

Back in our fifth floor hotel room, even more ladybugs had come onboard. What was going on?

This time Elliot ushered the ladybugs down to the lobby and out the door to freedom, just as I had.

By the time he returned, one more had made an appearance. Realizing this could be a never-ending saga, we let it be. The way they all got in, they would also get out. But, I took solace that the ladybugs' visit had not been at random. They were on a mission. I knew ladybugs are a sign of good fortune and a wish fulfilled.

But, more was to come.

Our first morning back home, synchronicity played a hand. I had been working on a spiritual discipline called Practicing the Presence. After breakfast, I had remembered to invite the Christ to join me as I washed the dishes.   With my hands in a sink full of water, something made me look up at the kitchen windowsill. Mom's JUNE Birthday Angel had a little ladybug hand painted on the statue's base.

Why hadn't I seen it before?

In that God wink, I felt Mom's smiling presence.

Had the ladybugs been her way of getting me to see the big

picture? Even though I missed her in the physical, her love was forever with me. My spirits lifted. The ladybugs had fulfilled my wish to know that Mom was happy in heaven.

Several years later, I learned the ladybug's name in Spanish means "little Mary," and in German they are called "Mary's beetle." I couldn't help but smile as Mom's name was Mary Luckie.

~A Quantum Leap~

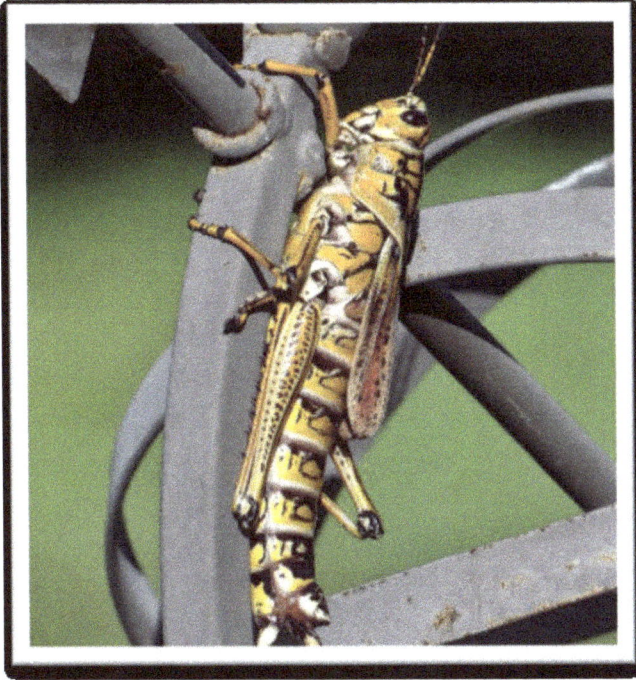

Remember, of course,
the song of the grasshopper, as well as the ant or bee—
but know in Whom ye have believed. For He,
the Giver of all good and perfect gifts,
has given these—the handiwork of His creation—
as a pattern or example or lesson, that ye—too—may learn.
--EDGAR CAYCE Reading 1965-1

One morning after a full moon lunar eclipse, I was watering the flowers when another phenomenon appeared in our front yard. A strange giant grasshopper had all the markings of ancient Egypt in his golden jeweled design. Basking in the sun. even more striking was his unusual pose on an old iron astrolabe in the flower garden.

Knowing a grasshopper can symbolize a major leap forward, this little astronomer was sending out a message of something far greater. His spindly legs seemed to be directing the long metal arrow on the vintage ornament, aiming it for the stars. His quantum leap prediction was on target as an astrolabe was once an instrument for scientists to measure the altitudes of celestial bodies.

Seeing his posturing somehow instilled an inner knowing that this was true for humanity. The chaotic transformational energies over the past years were hopefully bringing our evolution into a realm far beyond our current comprehension.

I ran for my camera to capture the moment, hoping he wouldn't take off. But it seemed I needn't have worried, because he was still there, holding his heavenly marker.

Later, after uploading the photos, a close-up view revealed more depth, those eyes seemed to hold a wisdom beyond this world.

Rather than be content to nibble on my rose bushes, he had come with a proclamation: To think on a much grander scale, to look beyond everyday appearances, to remember where we came from and where we would return. The celestial stars!

It is interesting to note that grasshoppers have an instinct for being in the warmth and light, and they know when to take a leap. They always make a leap up or forward, never backward, so when one appears on your path it indicates there will be no reversals. It's time to trust your own inner instincts and get ready to take a new leap forward. Progress!

Sometime later, a nature friend identified my "sighting" as a Florida lubber. Because of its short wingspan, this species can't fly. But that news made my messenger even more significant. No earthly limitations stopped my little land lubber from aiming beyond his realm. And, so can I, knowing my true heritage as a spiritual being.

~The Circle of Life~

Until he extends the circle of his
compassion to all living things,
man will not himself find peace.
--ALBERT SCHWEITZER

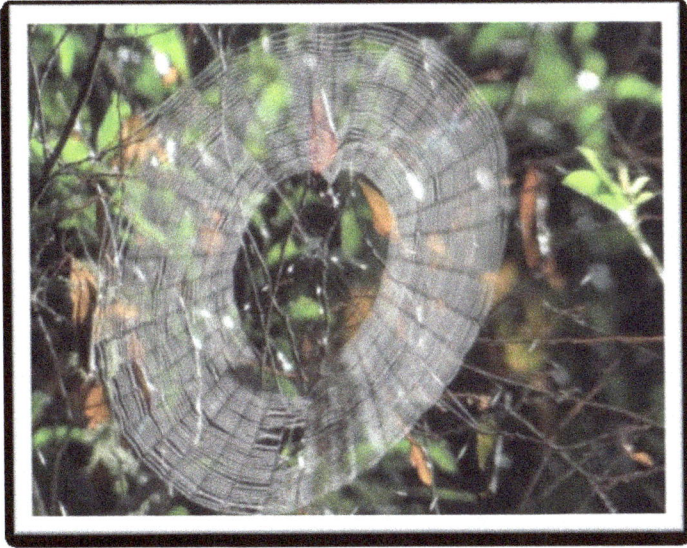

Nature is always communicating with us, often in ways we don't understand. Sometimes the radiant sun or luminescent moon, the Light will reveal a message that dispels our darkness. An ordinary event can catch us off guard, and cause a personal change of heart. The detailed gift speaks to our healing, bringing clarity and greater understanding—and, what blesses one, benefits all.

I have always loved the trees wherever I have lived. Just seeing them outside my window has been comforting. At one time, I had entertained the idea of moving, abandoning the beautiful sanctuary we co-created with nature. Instead, I chose to focus on peace, not what my five senses were telling me about so-called reality. The Introduction to *A Course in Miracles* helped me: "Nothing real can be threatened, nothing unreal exists, therein lies the peace of God."

A spiritual newsletter also arrived in the mail that addressed an issue regarding the destruction of my neighbor's trees. I could not understand what had possessed my good neighbor to cut down so many trees. The newsletter helped me see what we humans perceive as a tree, is not really the tree at all, but our mental concept of a tree. The world we see dwells in a mental realm, but in truth, trees are spiritual ideas, held in eternal perfection, regardless of outer appearances.

I surrendered my sadness in the midst of chaos and chose to focus on peace instead, appreciating the life of the remaining ancient hardwoods that poured into the sky outside my window.

Early one morning, in hopes of seeing the rare pedigree Super Moon, I ran to the den and opened the curtains.

I was not disappointed.

Although the rare lunar orb remained hidden, an even more wondrous circle glistened in the sun's rays.

An industrious spider had strategically woven her handiwork above the mourning pile of my neighbor's felled trees.

I recognized this beautiful strong web had been woven with a message from nature. Not trusting my eyes, I zoomed in with my camera over the fence to make sure I was seeing what I thought I was seeing.

Woven with deliberate intensity, the spider had spared no effort in her creativity, tirelessly weaving round and round. My spirit leaped as I began to notice that nature was rebounding. Massive heart shaped vines had covered the "resting" trees in a blanket of green leaves. With tear-filled eyes, I saw how thick tree stumps now burst in leafy thick bushes. New life. Resurrection energy.

That radiant circle was like a whisper to me: *All life is sacred. All life is in this web together joined by one continuous fine silk thread. What harms one, harms all. What blesses one, blesses all. This finite circular design is a symbol of infinity, with no beginning and no ending. So bring love and peace to this fragile union, honor it by your every thought, word, and action. You are the creator of your destiny by what you weave into your life.*

The touch of nature had been so unexpectedly healing. Later I looked out the window once more. The morning sun had shifted; the Circle of Life now hidden in the recesses of nature, but joyfully illumined in my mind.

~The Trumpet Swan~

As a child, I loved *The Ugly Duckling* by Danish author Hans Christian Andersen. As the story goes, a small bird born in a barnyard is badly treated by the others around him until he matures into the most beautiful bird of all, a swan. In this inspiring tale of personal transformation, swan is a symbol of awakening to the true beauty and power of the Self. Not only seeing it in ourselves, but learning to recognize it in others.

The message came close to home when this beautiful white swan showed up at the park, as beautiful and striking as a fairy tale. It was the spring of 2015 and I was going through some major challenges. Her beauty and grace were refreshing to my soul as I watched her glide through rippled waters, she was the heart of the lake. Curious, a little research pointed out swans don't typically like hot weather, and she had arrived in the company of a another northern bird I'd yet to see in Florida—one of my favorites, a Canadian goose. A recent storm had perhaps caused the unlikely couple to seek refuge at the lake, but their visit was not at random.

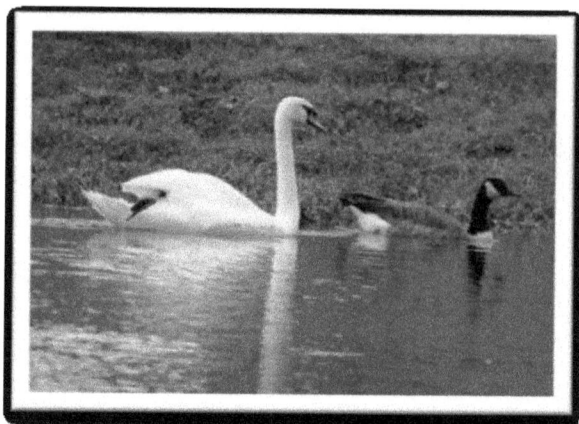

When swan appears, it can signal magical realms are opening up. An exciting time to trust and follow your true Self and share your creativity. New opportunities will be coming your way just as the white trumpet swan had suddenly appeared out of nowhere with no human help.

The message was double as I knew a Canadian goose signals it's time to heed the call to the quest and to follow your heart. Goose also is about writing. The swan's partner took off after a few weeks to return to his flock. But the beautiful swan remained through the spring, summer and fall, and we enjoyed visiting her often. One day my camera captured an unexpected sight: a beautiful pyramid of light appeared on her white feathery body as she preened in the sunshine. By humbly bowing her head, the shadows of her neck had framed the illumining symbol.

It seemed so deliberate that I wondered about the significance. Curious, I looked up the word pyramid. One definition seemed like a fit: to increase rapidly step by step on a broad base. I liked that image of light as the building block.

The message I gleaned from our beautiful trumpet swan seemed to herald a time for us to humbly bow our heads and listen within our hearts. Reach for the highest spiritual experiences so that your inner light will be turned outward and the shadows will fade into lightness of being.

~The White Peacock~

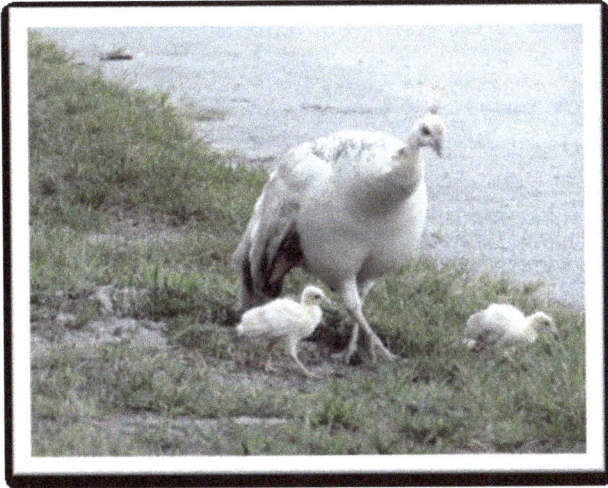

A rehab center not far from home is nestled in nature where a family of peacocks have taken up residence in the woods. One evening visiting a friend in recovery due to a fall, I was hoping to get a glimpse of the beautiful peacocks on the grounds. Almost dusk, as I walked to the car, an angel message came to drive up the hill rather than exit by the fence where they sometimes perch. I recalled an amusing time when a family of five were on the fence, side by side with their folded plumage draped like long pony tails. Regretfully, I didn't have my camera as their presence seemed to mirror an issue that I had been "on the fence about" for quite some time. I attribute that rare sighting to my getting off the fence and taking an appropriate action that had positive results.

Hoping to glimpse them again that evening, the angel guidance was again helpful as the royal blue peacock family had just crossed the road, and I watched them strut up the sloping hill, tails dragging. but I was too late for a photo op.

Just then, a new family emerged from the forest.

To my surprise, I saw a graceful white peacock with her three baby chicks! As I spoke softly to her about taking a picture, Mama seemed most cooperative and even posed, crossing her legs in an "X" as I zoomed in with gratitude.

Not having seen white peacocks on the premises, I was curious as to the symbolism. Later I learned the white peacock is aligned to the higher consciousness. It represents the most beautiful time of your life. A time when you have reached the point of embracing who you truly are; a spiritual being having a joyful physical life experience.

The symbolism matched the "X" as it is also a symbol for Christ. With Christ consciousness, ideas can hatch to lovingly share with others.

~It's a Wrap~

When you do things from your soul,
you feel a river moving in you, a joy.
--RUMI

(Baby squirrel outside my den window)

My writer friend, Joanna, inspired this book. Her suggestion had been to take my experiences from my nature angel blog angelforyou.org and create a book. Excited, I began the project, but things got in the way.

One hot day in the shade of the orange tree in the backyard, a squirrel scampered down and from a low branch above me he stared, chattering and flicking his tail, "giving me the business". I thanked him for his message. I had postponed my nature book long enough. It was time to let go and finish it.

From then on, it seemed that wherever I went a squirrel would appear. One morning, as I was journaling about the squirrel synchronicity, a bushy squirrel showed up winding his tail before taking a leap off a tall tree outside my den window.

I ran outdoors with my camera; I wanted a photo for the angel blog on squirrel energy. Elliot spotted another lone squirrel scurrying along the back fence, but my zoom was too slow to catch him. My ego chided, if only your reflexes were faster! Oh well, a cute squirrel on top of the Saint Francis statue was what I had in mind.

Like most things, when trying too hard, we come up short. Finally, I gave up. Weeding the garden, I made an intention that the perfect squirrel would show up; one that *wanted* to be in the angel nature blog.

Later while taking a break, I watched two squirrels playfully chase each other up and down a tall oak. Again, my zoom couldn't track their rapid pace and I began to wonder if I would ever get a photo?

I surrendered and went inside to write. At the computer, I heard a noise. Looking up at the den window, I'd found a winner! A baby squirrel was looking in the window at me, clinging to a high branch. *Here I am*, he seemed to say as he waited for me to get my camera focused. Zooming in, I thanked him for his cooperation.

It was a good lesson: *what is yours will come to you.* Just set your goals, ask for help, and then move on, do something different. The universe will fulfill your desire, when it involves serving, caring, and sharing with others.

~Making a Splash~

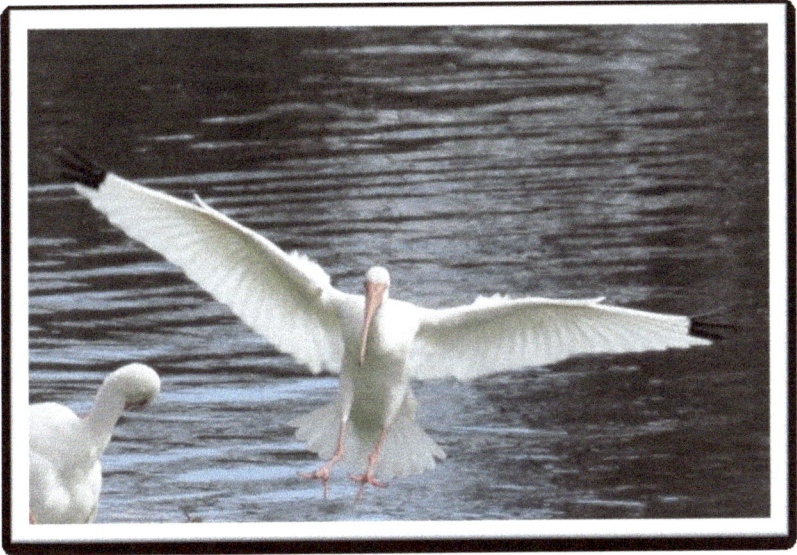

The past is over
and all that is left
is a blessing.
--A COURSE IN MIRACLES

The ibis was a symbol for the first letter in the ancient Egyptian alphabet and as such has a strong association with the written word. One in particular caught my attention at the park and was singled out when I uploaded my pictures. The lake was overflowing with flocks of these beautiful white wings, a flurry of long pink beaks and matching feet. Communication was in the air. Later, while enlarging the photos, it didn't seem as though I'd captured anything special, but a closer look revealed this happy ibis about to make a big splash. Wings tattered from recent storms, she was a picture of victory, landing feet first in the cool refreshing lake. I made it!

Her descent upon the waters brought to mind the sacred Book of Life. A reminder that each day a precious new page awaits our entry recorded by our every thought, word, and deed. The choice is ours to make a joyful splash into the new by being fully present in each moment.

About the Author

Rae Karen Hauck is the author of *Rise and Shine: A Spiritual Journey*, a student of *A Course in Miracles*, a Reiki Teacher, and an Angel lecturer. For three years she was a monthly volunteer speaker on the topic of Angels at the Association for Research & Enlightenment in Virginia Beach.

Her career as a supervisory management analyst with the Department of Defense changed direction when she decided to work with her brother, Rex Hauck, on a sequel to *Angels: The Mysterious Messengers*, an angel documentary that both aired on NBC.

Rae Karen lives in central Florida with her husband, Elliot, and Angel, their tuxedo cat. She enjoys communing with nature in her garden, photography, and sharing messages on her popular international **Angels for You blog**. www.angelforyou.org

Bibliography

Andrews, Ted. *Animal-Speak, The Spiritual and Magical Powers of Creatures Great and Small*. St. Paul, MN: Llewellyn Publications, 1995.

Andrews, Ted. *Nature-Speak: Signs, Omens and Messages in Nature*. Jackson, TN: Dragonhawk Publishing, 2004.

Boone, James Allen. *The Language of Silence*. New York, NY: Harper & Row, 1970.

Boone, James Allen. *Kinship with All Life*. New York, NY: Harper & Row, 1954.

Clark, Glenn. *The Man Who Talks with the Flowers*. St. Paul,   MN: Macalester Park, Publication Co., June 1976.

A Course in Miracles. Temecula, CA: Foundation for Inner Peace, 1975, 1985.

Kennedy, David Daniel. *Feng Shui for Dummies*. Hoboken, NJ: John Wiley & Sons, 2010.

Merton, Thomas. *New Seeds of Contemplation*. Bardstown, KY: Abbey of Gethsemani, Inc., 1961.

Meyer, Regula. *Animal Messengers: An A-Z Guide to Signs and Omens in the Natural World*. Rochester, Vermont: Bear & Co., 2012.

Nahmad, Claire. *Angel Messages: The Oracle of the Birds*. London. Watkins Publishing, 2010.

Sams, Jamie & Carlson, David. *Medicine Cards, The Discovery of Power*

Through the Way of Animals. Santa Fe, NM: Bear & Co., 1988.

www.ingramcontent.com/pod-product-compliance
Lightning Source LLC
Chambersburg PA
CBHW041922090426
42741CB00020B/3452